On The Back
OF THE
Wildebeest

The Healing Power of Creativity

Audrey C. Jolly RP, MA, OSRP

Creativity & Transformation Group

The Publisher
> Creativity & Transformation Group
> - An imprint of Canadian Outdoor Press
> Riverdale, Toronto, Canada.
> www.canadianoutdoorpress.ca

Title
> On The Back of The Wildebeest
> The Healing Power of Creativity

ISBN 978-1-7771539-2-2

Cover image by Audrey C. Jolly

Table of

Acknowledgements 3

Introduction 7

Chapter 1
Creativity and Impulse 15

Chapter 2
Creativity, Process vs Product... 39

Chapter 3
Creativity and Blocks - Defenders, Judges and Critics..... 55

Chapter 4
Creativity and Boundaries... 77

Chapter 5
Creativity and Trauma... 87

Chapter 6
Creativity and Anger 107

Chapter 7
Creativity and Fear.. 121

Chapter 8
Creativity and Shame, Blame and Guilt 143

Contents

Chapter 9

Creativity and Sorrow 161

Chapter 10

Creativity and Joy 173

Chapter 11

Creativity and Wholeness 183

Chapter 12

Creativity and Altered States 199

Conclusion 215

Endnotes

Eight Effort Actions - Rudolph Laban 219

Catherine Marrion on Gibberish 220

Recommended Resources 221

Related Short Stories

Material Witness 225

Wild State 228

Art 233

List of Exercises

Chapter 1 Exploring Impulse

The I That is Speaking 31

Chapter 2 Product vs. Process

Of The Inner Parts..42

Surrendering Weight 49

Lying down, Hand Lead in 3s 50

Hand over Hand Lead Through Space..............................51

The Telescope - Multi-Modal Exercise Movement, Art, Writing, Theatre 51

Chapter 3 Exploring Your Blocks

Welcoming Emotion - A Multi-Modal Approach 67

Physical

Wants, Needs, Desire — A Multi-Modal Inquiry 67

Rogue Body Parts 69

Drum Dialogue...69

Interviewing the Protector...70

Protecting the Vulnerable..70

Balance, Fall and Recovery 71

The Rant..71

The Troll and the Lamb..72

Visual Art   73

Tight Drawing 73

Meandering Line..73

Sponge Blotting 74

Soaked With Sadness 74

Writing

Judges Journal...74

Chapter 4 Exercises

Physical Boundary Inquiry - Personal Space...................81
Writing

Crossing Boundaries 82
Movement and Theatre

Needs and Response 83
Art

Exploring Boundaries 84

Chapter 5 Exploring Trauma

Writing

Body Paper...101
Variation - Voice Paper 102
Visual Art

Sculpture - Blindfolded Sculpting 103

Chapter 6 Exercises For Anger

Exploring Body Shapes - Twisted, Gnarled...................113
Effort Actions in Movement 115
Theatre - How Aggression Relates 117
Language - Anger/Need Inquiry 118

Chapter 7 Exploring Fear

5-4-3-2-1 Grounding Through the Senses 134
Breathe, Ground and Observe.......................................135
Physical

Live and Die..137

Expression of Fear 137

Exploring the Inner Critics...139

Chapter 8 Exploration of Shame

Physical Warm Up - Tense and Release.............................152

Movement

Gravity Inquiry — Hall of Shame 152

Physical Theatre - Group Shame 153

The Sounds of Shame 154

Writing

Expressions of Shame...154

Visual Art

Collage of Shame..157

Writing

Accuser and the Accused 157

Chapter 9 Exercises in Sorrow

Language

Expressions of Sorrow..167

Visual Art

Body Mapping 168

Movement and Sound

Physical Warm Up - Tension and Release 168

Ice to Vapour..168

Body Shapes..169

Sorrow Inquiry Through the Elements 170

Chapter 10 Creativity and Joy

Physical Inquiry into Joy

Embody Joy 176

Movement

Massage, Shake and Move..178

Writing 178
Visual Art
Expressions of Joy 179

Chapter 11 Exploring Wholeness

Writing
The Good, The Bad and The Ugly Inquiry 195
Blind Feelings 195
Visual Art
Perfect Flower Collage 196

Chapter 12 Exploring Altered States

Multi-Modal Exercise for Altered States 213

Acknowledgements

We've made it!

I am profoundly grateful to Sue Reynolds as editor and teacher who skillfully corralled the herd-of-cats that is my writing style. I couldn't have done it without her.

Thanks to the Buffleheads, my trusty writing cohorts who listened with patience and generosity, laughing in all the right places.

My first writing experience with Maureen Jennings, author of The Map of Your Mind, Journeys into Creative Expression, where I became a published poet, planted the seed that led to this book.

Marion Woodman and Elinor Dickson introduced me to feminine psychology through their generous soul offerings. Wendy Fredricks and Randi Helmers, who offer unwavering support embody SOPHIA, the sacred feminine.

Ed Horner, soul partner and friend, has danced with my scared and scary parts. He lovingly cracked the whip when needed, worked on design, content and has published and marketed this book, working tirelessly. Such an act of love. I'm so fortunate to have him by my side.

I am profoundly indebted to John Went, of the *Integral Healing Centre of Toronto* for his love and support. I wouldn't be a psychotherapist today without him.

Susan Aaron and Paul Hyckie of *Psychodramatic Bodywork* shared their knowledge and loving spirits in communities I call home.

Dr. Richard Schwartz and Sue McRae of *Internal Family System Therapy* have deepened my personal healing and therapeutic repertoire, offering a clear road map for the internal parts work. I thank Gennie Brukner and Sandra Flear, my beloved *Authentic Movement* family that share deep dives into infinite healing.

I also thank Emily Conrad and Kim Brodey for *Continuum*, an exquisite breath and body work I've been so privileged to study.

Physical theatre coaches - Linda Putnam, Deena Levy and most recently, Anita La Selva who encouraged me to be brave and show up big.

Clown teachers - Richard Pochinko and DeanGilmour invited me to leap into my fear, play around and break through to a bolder confidence.

Voice teacher – Richard Armstrong of Roy Hart Theatre, France opened creative worlds through his mentorship and collaboration at the Banff Centre, AB. I thank MaryAnn Jazvac and Catherine Marrion as my beta readers, Marian Wihak award-winning designer and artist for her eye on design, and Elinor Dickson, Maureen Jennings, Rona Maynard and Paula Thomson for their generous endorsements.

Pat Fairhead, artist/mentor/friend has provided the fodder for many adventurous stories. She consistently encourages my *wild child* to dance with bells on. Heidi Croot, with her keen editor's eye also listened and commiserated when I needed it most.

Finally, I thank Gayle Dempsey and Gary Froude of *Arts in Muskoka, the Muskoka Place Gallery* and *Muskoka Chautauqua* for their support of me as a visual and performing artist, teacher and author and the *Muskoka Authors Association* for turning me into an award-winning author.

Pause for a moment.
Don't try and be "spiritual."
Don't seek any particular state or feeling.
Just become aware of the very ordinary moment.
Drench it with awareness. Infuse it with curiosity.
If it's uncomfortable, let it be uncomfortable.
If it's heavy, let it be heavy.
If it's boring, let it be boring.
Leave the moment fully untouched,and let it touch you.
Awaken to the sacred ordinariness of things...

~ Jeff Foster

Introduction

The image of a Starling, a small bird that rides on the back of a Wildebeest, a buffalo-sized mammal, sets the visual stage for this book on creativity and trauma. A *Beauty And The Beast* story. The Starling represents our creative spirit and soul, the essence of freedom, while the beast, heavy and earthbound represents the body of trauma we carry beneath our conscious, everyday selves.

I define trauma as our emotional response to a deeply distressing or disturbing experience along with the body's unresolved response to it. Shock or denial are typical responses, with longer-term reactions being erratic, or explosive emotions, flashbacks, strained relationships, or a wide range of physical symptoms such as muscle tension or hyperactivity.

In the wild, the Starling lands on the Wildebeest, eating bugs and parasites that would otherwise bother the creature. The beast provides this buffet for the bird. The bird is able to perch and rest while eating. The bird serves the beast, and the beast serves the bird. Their relationship is symbiotic. They complement each other while contrasting: light to heavy, free to bound, known to unknown, relatively harmless to potentially threatening. The bird swoops and dips in space, while the beast is bound to the earth with its feet rooted in the dirt and grime.

In Greek mythology the wildebeest or *Catoblepas* was said to be a shaggy, sluggish creature with a heavy head that hung towards the ground. This was advantageous due to its deadly gaze. Anyone it fixed its bloodshot eyes upon would die immediately. It was said to emit fire from its nostrils and possess a lethal breath due to a diet of poisonous vegetation. This is a great metaphor for trauma, similar to Medusa, the winged female with living, venomous snakes in place of hair. Those who gazed into her eyes turned to stone. The Greeks could well have been using these metaphors to describe terrifying, unexplainable, traumatic events and the fear, shame and intensity surrounding them.

For me, the Wildebeest represents the body's unconscious trauma. Parts of us take on the role of carrying these traumas allowing us to function in the world. These hidden parts hold mysteries and riches for us to discover and embrace. They are the pathways to living a more integrated life.

A client once imagined her traumas were stored in bins that were stacked to the ceiling in a rental storage unit. Her everyday self was left pushing a wheelbarrow containing a pile of bones that was her skeleton self being pushed from place to place. As with any rental, there is a cost to carrying these internal storage units. Over time the physical, emotional and energetic costs go up, the available space decreases, leaving us with less room to breathe, move, create and dream.

The seed of this book took root during the completion of my Master's Degree at York University in the early '80s. I arrived from a small, tight-knit community of artists in Saskatoon, where I was well known as a teacher and performer, and entered York, a vast, sprawling place where no one knew me. The transition revealed a gaping crack in my psyche. Like Humpty Dumpty, I fell and shattered. And now I'm grateful for that. That younger self had her limitations. She struggled with anxiety and was overwhelmed much of the time. She felt lost.

In those days, I was 'performing' to the outside world as if I was 'just fine.' I was struggling to finish my thesis while teaching with the Dance, Phys Ed. and Grad Theatre Depts. One of the courses I was taking,was Dance Therapy; a requisite for being in that class was that we would undergo personal therapy. That simple requirement opened the door to a whole new world for me, leading to a rewarding new career as artist-healer.

In therapy, I discovered that I had stuffed parts of myself away from my everyday self that lived out in the world. It was a means of self-preservation, but to maintain the coverup, I had to lie, cheat, steal and deny as well as control and coerce myself and others around me into believing that I was a good person deserving of love and acceptance. Sounds like a lot of work? It was.

I believe most of us are working at least this hard much of the time to remain balanced on the tightrope of acceptability to ourselves and others. As I delved into these dark chambers of the shadow material that I was hauling around with me, I also discovered other parts of the self that were transcendent, otherworldly and spirited, full of creativity and mystery.

Theatre is said to be about *lying*, *cheating*, and *stealing*, so it offered a creative space for me to explore the various parts of the lost self. One must recognize those words without negativity attached, only playful inquiry. Through creativity, I was able to embrace the disowned parts and unite

9

them with my everyday self. Bold, new confidence arose out of "unpacking the shit" as I had at one time named it. Now I know it's the gold, the grit that forms the pearl in the oyster.

I made the transition from artist to teacher to therapist, each new career born from a series of breakthroughs that continue to this day. This book is one of those breakthroughs for me, a way of uniting the artist, teacher and therapist within and delivering a synthesized version of *'this is what I know about that.'*

My hope for the readers of this book is that there is an infusion of confidence and daring into their lives while waking up those sleeping or stored-away parts. These parts deserve to be heard, seen and mined for the richness they hold. These buried parts are calling us all of the time, physically, emotionally, creatively. We need to listen. Let's travel together to the deeper regions of the self and discover the gold. When you imagine a full-length magic mirror that reflects all the aspects of who you are, do you want to run and hide? Or do you feel genuinely excited and curious, ready to explore your deepest unknown parts through a variety of creative approaches?

I love the line, "I'm an open book you just don't know how to read." Our hidden parts could say that to us. Their modes of communication are often not familiar to us; they may be speaking as a bodily ache or pain, an emotional longing or a feeling that something's missing, without knowing what. If you're thinking "there must be more to life" you are correct! There are parts of you that are waiting, patiently, for you to come and find them. Once they are released from their hiding places and are free to express themselves, you gain more access to creativity, happiness and health.

The parts that you least like in yourself are the parts that most need your curiosity, acceptance and assistance — this, in turn, provides fuel for passion, creativity and healing. By reading this book and engaging with the exercises, I hope to convince you of that truth. I will share with you stories of how these lost and scared parts of the self are found, helped and healed. I will draw upon personal anecdotes as well as the experiences of my clients and students.

To supplement the stories, I offer creative and emotional support, by reframing and refining your ideas and approach to the whole self and suggest practical exercises to help you get started on the path to freedom and wholeness.

I also share techniques to help build the bravery and confidence needed to tackle inner critics, judges, and intense emotions you will inevitably meet along the way. Giving creative expression to these scared and wounded parts frees them of the traumas they carry both energetically and emotionally. We must never underestimate the power of creativity and its capacity to heal us, but we must also have a road map with us indicating the pitfalls and cracks in the road with a users guide 'for what to do next.' Through this book, I hope to show you the unlimited creative possibilities as well as some of the dips and curves in the road that you might encounter.

The Body of the Book – the What, Why and How

The book begins with my definition of creativity; that which is new and unknown. The nature of creating means that we are in uncharted territory and therefore not likely that comfortable. As humans, it's our nature to lean towards that which is familiar, allowing us to feel comfortable and safe.

To depart from our comfort zone, we need to have particular resources in place. These resources have to do with our thoughts, beliefs, emotions and sensations. We need to know how to steer our intellects, challenge our beliefs (many are obsolete) and, most importantly, be able to tolerate our felt sensations.

Much of my work as a body-based psychotherapist is helping clients learn to tolerate their felt sensations—what they are feeling in the body. Those felt sensations may feel negative, even in positive situations. The nervous system may register threat where there isn't any. Intimacy and pleasure can trigger an uncomfortable sensation in the body, as easily as pain and suffering.

An exploration into the unknown parts of the self, while supporting the potentially fearful parts that may surface in the process, is an art form in itself. Permission to enter is required of the inner protectors before they will let down their guard, allowing you to respond to impulses without scrutiny or a shutting down. As with a bird or a squirrel in a tree nearby, one fast move on your part and they're gone.

Through experimentation and observation, we can learn our unique defence style, what we require of ourselves to allow entry into our vulnerable, creative selves. The treasures that await discovery are unimaginable.

You have a unique voice and a unique path. This book helps to define your path through a multi-disciplinary approach with exercises at the end of each chapter that you can mix and match for the best fit for you. If you prefer writing, do the writing exercises. If you wish to branch out into movement, drama or visual art, you can do that. You don't need previous experience in any of the arts to work the process, only a curious mind and support for yourself if fears arise.

This book also offers aid in addressing those fears right off the bat with helping strategies. It's a process-versus-product approach. In our creative practice, as artists, we often focus on the end result and not the moment that we are in; this stifles the creative impulse and limits our possibilities.

In Chapters 5–8 we drill down into the specifics of healing through creativity, addressing core emotions of anger, fear, sorrow as well as deeper body level explorations of joy and discovering what wholeness is. In Chapter 9 we explore altered states of consciousness we can find ourselves in where the thin veil of one reality opens into other realities.

I hope that this book becomes a companion for you on an adventurous journey in search of your complete self. Through this process, you will find healing and a new sense of freedom and wholeness. You can discover a unique capacity to embrace the detours and difficult passages with a freshness and strength that comes from your new and enhanced creative toolkit. I encourage you to welcome all that you meet of yourself along the way with curiosity, compassion and creative permission and know you will become brave and bold in the process. I believe you will learn to handle the inner critics and transform them into wacky characters, wild paintings and prophetic poems.

Let the creative journey begin!

Chapter 1

Creativity and Impulse

I stood before a class of fourth year dancers at York University and asked them to move across the room in a way that was interesting to them.

They looked puzzled. "What do you mean?" They wanted me to tell them what to do and show them how to do it.

I said, "If I show you, it will be my way and not yours."

I asked them to close their eyes, go inside and find a way to move that was satisfying and uniquely theirs. They were at a loss. I had my work cut out for me. For decades these students had danced to copy their teachers, without connecting to what was inside of them.

I understood this. I had been one of those dancers.

I've met many actors, visual artists, musicians and therapists who are disconnected from inner impulse and their authentic selves. Generally in classes and workshops we are taught by the "monkey see, monkey do" approach to life. We are not taught how to connect with ourselves or given the emotional safety and support necessary to make that connection possible.

Being a teacher often conveys a sense of superiority and judgement. Authentic impulses in students don't dare reveal themselves. Instead, these spontaneous impulses burrow deep inside, and remain there to stay safe.

A lifetime of external threat (that often begins before any formal teaching situation) creates an inner dynamic where we judge and shame ourselves while fearing others. As a result, our impulses and authentic selves aren't safe with us, let alone with anyone else. Repairing the internal relationships between different parts of the self is an important first step to regaining connection with the authentic self.

These internal relationships often reflect external ones we've had in the past. A negative, critical parent may have created an internal negative part that judges the vulnerable self harshly. Understanding where these patterns of behaviour began helps in repairing, and ultimately shifting them, from negative and judgmental to more positive and supportive.

Sadly, we are often taught to disconnect from the spontaneous, authentic self at a very early age in our families, schools, churches and communities. To regain this authentic self is to open up worlds of creative/emotional, healing potential. There would be a much happier, healthier world if emotional safety and freedom to explore creatively were more present in the early childhood experience.

We often behave towards the self in ways that we would never think of behaving towards a friend—nor would a friend likely let us get away with it—we'd be friendless. But we behave badly to ourselves and seem to believe that it's OK. We may even think we deserve it. What a misconception! We couldn't be more wrong!

As human beings, we are tribal. Belonging to the group means we are safer; exclusion means increased danger or threat. We have a great need to belong, to feel accepted and loved. To protect ourselves, we hide, play it safe, don't take risks, and don't let ourselves be vulnerable, free and joyful—all because of a fear of looking stupid or flawed or weird and being ostracized as a result. Most of the time, we walk around worried about how much of our 'real self' is showing. We fear embarrassment, shame, and humiliation. Experiencing those emotions felt horrible as a child or teen; our adult lives are spent attempting to ward off any further embarrassment at all cost.

A lack of physical safety or emotional support from others contribute to small, tense, tight living. We play it safe or scramble for worthiness, we beg for belonging. Abandonment and abuse create an environment where a child learns these survival patterns.

I lived in fear of "being seen" for a great deal of my early life. Only later in life, through clown, physical theatre, *Authentic Movement*, and therapy, was I able to emerge and be seen without feeling judged, shamed or abandoned.

At the time I didn't consciously know what I lacked. I had a sense that something was missing but I couldn't identify what. My personality had formed around wounds and traumas, conditioned by fragile attachments and unsafe surroundings. I had developed coping mechanisms and adaptations to keep myself safe. Because of this, I couldn't really connect with my authentic self.

It wasn't until much later in life that I discovered inner impulse work, which I then refined through years of *Authentic Movement*, clown and theatre improvisation. There I developed a body-level confidence that came from listening and responding to impulse, that allowed for spontaneity and freedom.

I took this impulse work into painting and then writing. I began to discover aspects of myself and build inner relationships with parts that longed for expression. In this process, I could face the fear, insecurity and shame that I had accumulated over a lifetime. I strengthened my confidence to create and express. I found teachers and therapists who could help me find more of my lost selves. I began to piece together the whole self. In return, in my work as a teacher, coach and therapist, I was able to help others do the same.

The term "impulse," as I'm using it here, is that spontaneous, in-the-moment response that occurs in relation to one's creativity, where the art-maker is truly present, uncensored, and able to listen and observe inwardly and freely respond and express. It requires a confidence and sense of self-worth that allows one to be seen in all aspects of the self, by the self and by others.

If you don't yet connect with your inner creative self, that's OK too—you are welcome here. There's a place for you. I'm happy you're here.

The inner creative self has a mind of its own. One that is quite different from the everyday self. It exists in a different reality. It does different work, thinks differently, approaches the moment in a non-linear way. Your "everyday self" or the "functional self," is the self that lifts the food from your plate to your mouth, buys the groceries and drives to work.

Emilie Conrad from *Continuum,* a breath and body practice, called this self the 'fetch wood, carry water' self.

My understanding of impulse has come through many practices; creative movement, *Continuum, Authentic Movement*, theatre and vocal, improv, clown, art and writing. Meditation is a practice that can uncover impulse but may be too stationary a practice for some.

Whether you are connecting inward in stillness, responding in movement or interacting with others, the ability to connect and respond to impulses as they appear from within, adds to the spontaneity and vitality of one's life, creatively and socially.

The impulse work one does in one area of creativity influences other areas too. For example my movement or theatre work with impulse, affects my painting and writing practice; my writing and painting became more spontaneous and bold, freer with more options available in any one moment. I learned to trust the nudge of impulse with less fear or attachment to outcome. I'm less invested in how the artwork looks or how I look or sound.

Discovering Impulse in Writing

As I set out to write this instructional book on creativity, and the body's role in psychotherapy and healing, a strange thing began to occur. As I wrote along from my mostly right-brain memory recall (based on facts, research and findings as a teacher and psychotherapist) 'rogue' ideas began to pop up, left of centre, clearly 'other' from the context of the linear direction my writing was going in.

"Stop it! Go away! Stop distracting me. You're not appropriate. You don't fit here," were some of the knee jerk responses I had to the appearance of these fleeting rogues.

19

They would disappear as fast as they appeared, for a while anyway. But I consistently felt a tug on my sleeve, distracting my forwards thinking and organized trains of thought. My curiosity for these 'rogue' distractions grew over time and I found my attention lingering longer with them as they slipped in, brushing up against my arm or nibbling at my elbow, hovered over my ear or tickled my nose. They caused me to smile at times and raise an eyebrow in surprise at other times.

I decided to listen and welcome these rogues, these tangents. As I carried on with my writing, my focus shifted to what was popping up, seemingly out of nowhere, and taking me on a romp into the deeper recesses of my mind, my psyche, my body, my emotions away from what I had set out to do.

Some of these dark recesses and corners of my mind hadn't been dusted out in a very long time, maybe never. These tangents, these unusual risings or appearances became rich and revealing of so many lost aspects of myself.

Since I was hand writing in a notebook I began sticking these impulses – these marginal thoughts – in the margins of my notebook. Later, after I'd completed the thought I was exploring, I could return to them and pick them up.

I found these peripheral thoughts were often more interesting and personally engaging than the writing path I was on at the time. My challenge was to stick to a specific path or train of thought until the subject was complete before pursuing the lure of a tangent.

This awareness of impulse in writing is a longstanding process for me. During my thesis in Interdisciplinary Studies at York University in Dance and Psychology, I was using an instrument to measure teacher-student interactions and, once again, things started popping up that I was observing that my instrument didn't measure.

"What do I do with this?" I asked. "Drop it? Disregard it? Ignore it? I need to stick to the path I've set out on that will undoubtedly prove my hypothesis for my paper. But should I follow my curiosity, and inquire further into these observations?"

These aberrations seemed to have a bit more juice and allure than the observations gathered by the instrument that I was using to measure interactions in the classroom during a creative dance class.

My thesis committee didn't get what I was talking about with the findings. But in the end, they allowed me to publish them in a chapter of my thesis titled "meta-discussion." This section was where I could gather and discuss the unexplainable, immeasurable, non-factual, or subjective findings. In other words–the juicy bits–the seedlings for future explorations that would lead to professional careers and eventually this book.

I highly recommend this cross-pollination for anyone who wishes to take their creativity to another level. I'm a better psychotherapist for having done movement and theatre. The bravery I gained from doing movement and theatre I love to share with others. We can develop the confidence and courage to be vulnerable, look silly or ridiculous, even play through shame and humiliation transforming it from a discomfort to a strength.

My strongest, earliest and most consistent practice of following impulse has been through *Authentic Movement*. I have gathered in groups of movers, eyes closed, responding to movement and sound impulses for decades. I trained as an instructor and taught it for many years.

Working with actors, we brought in cameras, recorded the sessions and studied them, creating choreographies from the footage we gathered. There were moments when everyone was moving in perfect harmony with each other even though all eyes were closed and no one knew it was happening, other than the group's instructor. Some people moved a lot while others sat quietly, moving very little. There is not right way or wrong response.

Of all the creative work I've done over the past four decades, clown was an area of study that challenged me the most. It's deeply connected to impulse and it's done in front of an audience, upping the pressure.

Clowns are often *'In the shit'* - caught in the wrong place at the wrong time, doing the wrong thing. Visibility is at its height when you are out on stage as a clown, baring your soul. One exhausts all the familiar responses, and you are caught, stripped naked, without anything to fall back on. There is no place to hide. That moment is the clown's potent space where everything is on the line: inner balance, identity, confidence and comfort. It's a space between the *'panic and possibilities'* where the possibilities are infinite. Here is where a baby clown is born.

Impulses then rise out of the unconscious with a freshness and spontaneity that can shock and surprise everyone including one's self. It's some of the scariest and most exhilarating work I've done both as an artist and teacher.

For example, one dramatic scenario for a clown 'turn' might be that you are a janitor at the Metropolitan Opera House. You are back stage cleaning the floor and you stumble out onto the stage only to find the auditorium is full of an anticipatory audience waiting for the Peking Opera to begin. You are royally *'in the shit'*. How you respond in that moment is often very surprising to you as well as your audience. There is a certain amount of anxiety and fear present for the performer in those moments and responses can be widely varied. You might freeze or pretend you aren't actually there—which is rather funny since you are painfully visible. Unpredictable responses often fly out in these moments. I've seen clowns fake operatic scenes from the Mikado with audiences that laughed so hard they fell from their seats and rolled on the floor.

I studied clown with many extraordinary teachers such as Richard Pochinko, Dean Gilmour, Jim Warren and Rickie Wolf.

I have many memorable moments, but one that stands out for me was during an end-of-term performance in Richard Pochinko's class. I had developed a clown turn that had a stuffed budgie bird in a covered cage and a sound box that tweeted from inside the cage as well. Walking out on stage to perform, the budgie dropped from the covered cage, quite by accident, to the floor. My entire plan for the show was lost in that moment. I was truly, "in the shit." What to do? I remained in the moment of a shocking dilemma and (luckily) knew to keep my connection with the audience. But what now? Do I ignore the bird on the floor and carry on as if it didn't happen? Do I try to subtly brush the bird off to the side while distracting the audience elsewhere or pick it up and begin CPR on its tiny bird chest in an attempt to revive it back to life?

On top of it all the bird sound was still chirping from inside the covered cage as if the bird was still alive. That was another problem to be dealt with. If I stayed still enough I could pretend there was no bird but when I moved in the slightest way and the bird sound activated. I responded as if a dart had pierced my gut. The audience roared. The more they roared the less I had to do and just the anticipation of my discomfort brought the house down. It was a clown's heavenly moment, all spontaneous play discovered in real time. It doesn't get much better than that.

It was a highlight of my career as a clown and performer. I was in 'the zone' where I could do no wrong. There's nothing quite like it when you get into that space as an artist. Heightened oneness I call it; a perfect flower moment (*Noh Theatre*) that I describe in Chapter 10.

But I had to have done my personal work to get to where I could expose the vulnerable core self. I had to tackle a core belief that said it isn't safe to be seen, it's better to hide and pretend. Only then one can play at pretending to hide while revealing real feelings.

We don't know what we don't know. Hearing 'you are so much more than you know' is just a mental concept until you have the the bodily experience of the 'more.' Having the physical, emotional experiences that actually change the brain chemistry and body experience is imperative or it's all remains words.

Clown work confronts our fears by revealing aspects of the self that we work very hard to hide from the outer world and ourselves. With the encouragement of responding to impulse, parts of the self absolutely fly out of their hidden closets. Sound scary? It is. But the level of impulse and parts of the self we connect with in this work is unmatched. Exploring impulses in *Authentic Movement*, where your eyes are closed and you aren't in front of an audience, feels much safer. Clown is much riskier and the rewards can be much greater. Riding the wave of such impulse work is well worth exploring.

I want to mention here, however, that there's a difference between creative risk and actual risk and physical to one's safety. While the former is the heart of a true creative practice, the latter doesn't belong in artistry.

In Calgary, I worked on a play, *The Colour of Coal*. I was hired as a movement coach to work with six cast members in non-speaking roles who played the walls of the coal mine while other actors, with speaking roles, played the miners. With their bodies, sounds and hand instruments, the non-verbal actors created the physical and auditory living sense of the mine; the treacherous, life-taking tension in which miners worked and too often gave their lives. To build this team dynamic, I took them into the bowels of the building and did *bouffon* with them.

Bouffon is a term coined in the 1960s by Jacques Lecoq at his theatre school in Paris. Among other traits, it describes a clown style that mocks, is darker, often more gross than usual.

I had a hand drum. They banded together as outcasts—unwanted and at risk of harm—skulking around in the dimly lit industrial surroundings of pipes and boilers and storage bins. Garbage bags full of crumpled newspapers were scattered throughout the space giving the actors further places to hide under or toss about without injury.

The silence was palpable, the atmosphere threatening. Everyone hid and moved around, guarding all sides for potential danger. The tension built, there was threat at every corner. They had to navigate from one end of the building to the other. If I tagged anyone, with a light touch, they disappeared or fell to the ground in stillness representing death. With the drum I jumped out of the darkness from a corner or sounded off in the distance, coming closer and closer until they scattered in all directions, hiding separately then reuniting when it was safe to do so. The fear they experienced in their bodies was real, but the context was safe and everyone knew that. Because it wasn't a real-life situation of danger they were able to feel it, live it more fully in the body.

As an audience member watching live theatre or film we are able to lean into the experience, feeling the emotion it stirs in us. We know it's not real, so we are safe to experience our emotions more deeply. Entertainment activates our emotions within a safe container.

Emilie Conrad described *Continuum* as "lessons in making love with yourself." Can we bring a totally open curiosity and inquiry to the process, welcoming and inviting more without judging ourselves or needing any particular outcome to appear or be produced? We have bodies full of impulses that are occurring constantly; intellectual, physical, emotional, energetic, creative and spiritual. These impulses occur inside the self within the relationships of various parts. They also occur in our relationship to the world around us and into spiritual realms as well.

It's the impulses and the urges, the twitches and the tugs, the longings and the repulsions, the feelings and sensations that are the language of the body. The body is chattering, begging or screaming at us for our attention constantly. We ignore, shun, vanquish, and banish many of its cries for attention the moment they appear and experience them as an annoying inconvenience to our busy, otherwise preoccupied, day.

I often say in my office, *"Imagine that part of you that is feeling so lost or sad or distressed and anxious is a five-year-old child in your care, what would you do?"*

Or I ask, *"What if your daughter felt that way? What would you do or say to her, or to your best friend?"*

"Oh, that's easy, I would..." Clients are able to connect to an instant gut response that is healthy, loving and protective.

"Then why do you not give the same loving response to yourself when you feel the same way?" I ask.

26

The answer is often, *"I don't know,"* or *"It's not the same."*

We abandon our selves regularly, suppressing impulses, feelings and sensations in the body to control our behaviour. Some of this may be required, of course, to live in society as civilized beings but we go overboard with it. We mould ourselves into the shape of a person we think we need to be to prove to the world that we are lovable, deserving of respect and connection. We sellout the self for safety and connection. Most of it is an unconscious act.

I'm frequently asked the question, *"How do I get back to myself?"*

It's simple. Begin by listening.

We need to slow down and block out the noise and busyness if we are to listen and connect with the body in order to sense impulses. These impulses are happening all the time. We can track them and encourage them to unfold in real time. They will lead us someplace new and unpredictable. This is the edge of creation itself.

Creativity, in its essence, takes us into uncharted territory and is often scary. This work develops courage in dealing with the unknown as we expand into deeper experiences and richer artistic realms. Becoming excited and curious when we find we're in a new and unfamiliar place, is vital for an artist's process.

What is Impulse?

Impulses are spontaneous firings that may or may not motivate an action or a series of actions that follow any particular moment in time. They may occur on various levels: physical, emotional, energetic, spiritual or intellectual.

I deliberately leave the intellect to the end of that list as it generally dominates our lives already. We have become "top heavy" – relying too much on the intellect and not enough on our physical, emotional and spiritual selves. Our reasoning faculties need to be given a break from all the heavy work they do for us. Too much 'thinking' blocks creativity, pleasure and ease in the body. The intellect is a very important level of awareness but needs to be placed in proper balance with other aspects of our being. Let's give it a well-deserved rest.

We don't know what we're missing as most of us haven't lived integrated lives. As children we may feel the longing and lack of self but not be able to do much about it due to our age and circumstance. As adults we may have heard that we can change our bodies, emotions, spirit, energy and thoughts but we don't know how to follow through with it.

The more complicated question is 'how.' Our programming tells us to stay with the familiar, and what is familiar is often limited to what keeps us safe. But the pathways to living with more integration are always there if one knows how to spot them and follow their cues.

The cues are not linear. The intellect will try to make them make sense. It will question their value or significance, want to flit off to another thought that it finds more interesting or relevant rather than engaging with curiosity and inquiry, inviting "more please" to the sensations and impulses as they unfold. Developing a capacity to be present, and remain with the subtleties of the impulses takes time and practice.

Breath and the body work can bring us into the present. The *present moment* is all we have. The rest is hypothetical or memory, both sketchy at best and capable of sending us into a tailspin.

Being able to observe the physical body patterns we fall into is helpful. For instance, as I'm writing this, I notice that my spine curls forwards as my concentration increases. I'm unaware of it until the physical tension becomes uncomfortable. That's the language of the body speaking to me at this moment through tension, and discomfort. I pause my work, stretching into a back arch, finding release. This process may seem elementary and obvious because it's so automatic for us. Yet, I see so many people who are missing the obvious connection of these sensations with the body telling us something we need to know about the moment.

In theatre, there is a saying, "I'll do it but I won't watch" This beautifully describes one of these many internal disconnects that we have. It says, "I will do this move or this line or feel this feeling and express it, but I won't bear witness to myself as I do it. I can strip naked while at the same time recede into hiding within myself so no one can see me." We do this in many situations in life.

Right now if you pause what you are doing and take your attention to your physical body you might notice an impulse to stretch or twist or massage or move a certain way. You might notice that your body would like to shake or sigh or blow out air. Until you deliberately bring your attention to noticing these impulses, however, they remain unnoticed and unappreciated. Over time, on a physical level, these tensions become more rigid and set in permanent postures.

Sometimes these impulses come as an unwinding and releasing of gathered tension but not always. Starting with what feels tense is always good. I used to say in theatre every drop of tension holds an infinite supply of creative impulses. We don't want to get rid of our tension—we want to mine it for its potent creative content.

29

Find tension in your body; place a hand or hands on it, give it recognition, ask yourself what you are storing in it, breathe into it, move with it and sound from it.

Explore its emotional content; is it grief, anger, joy, fear, disappointment, or something else? Fake it till you make it. Try various possibilities—explore freely allowing yourself a broad playing field. Give yourself full permission to get it wrong—multiple times if you need to or not get it right at all. Those thoughts and feelings are only thoughts and feelings anyway. Let all be welcome. None are wrong. There are no mistakes.

Physical impulse can be more of a deliberate exploration that seeks kinaesthetic awareness. How do these muscles, tendons, connective tissues or bones move?

We can try imitating the way a baby engages with its newly discovered fingers, exploring what they can do. This is an approach of 'innocence,' rediscovering the body's capabilities. But we could also try an approach of 'experience', following impulses in the current-age body or even imaginatively at a future age—ten, twenty or thirty years down the road. Are you stiff so the impulse is to stretch or shake to loosen? Or are you antsy and jittery so the impulse is to hold and rock or curl up and squeeze in tight?

An exploration of physical impulse can bring us into the present moment and into connection with what's here now. This may include what was present in the past that we still carry in the body, what is here now or what will be here in the future based on the patterns that we have developed. The more we become aware of our physical patterns, tensions or weaknesses, overworked or underworked muscles, the more we are able to build balance and stability where energy flows more freely.

30

The same principles apply to emotional balance. If we are centred and grounded or know how to get back to our centre if we become ungrounded, we can go into deeper exploration. We choose what is working for us in the present and what is not. We gather or release what is necessary for our greatest good. By combining imagination and physical impulse we connect with emotion, spirit and soul. This opens the possibility of living a fuller, more vital life.

Now that we've established an understanding of impulse and its relationship to creativity let's bring it into the body through the following exercises. Remember, there is not one correct way to get there only your unique way. Feel free to wander off if the impulse arises, then return to the map if and when it serves you best.

Chapter 1 Exploring Impulse

The I That is Speaking

1. Find a comfortable position to put your body in. It might be lying on the floor or sitting or on all fours (hands and knees) however you are most comfortable. Let your body find the best spot for you today rather than deciding from your intellect. This might surprise you. We need to get the physical body back on line, communicating clearly to us. Say to yourself, silently or out loud, "I have a physical body" and then give yourself a set period of time (5 or 7 minutes to begin with, building up to longer) observing your physical body.

You might find that the first level of exploring physical impulse is recognizing where you are holding tension and deliberately letting it go. If you didn't get any further than that it would still be time well spent.

31

But if, after you have completed the exercise of letting go on a physical level, you find another level of physical impulse showing up that isn't driven from an awareness of tension and letting go, then Bravo! You are well on your way to exploring new worlds of physical impulse.

These various levels of impulse are all interconnected. An impulse in one realm may spark another impulse on a different level. For example you might be exploring physical impulses only to have emotional impulses appear. That's fine; allow all impulses to be there without blocking them. Recognize each impulse for what it is, arriving from any level of awareness; physical, emotional, intellectual, creative, energetic or spiritual, and then return to the level you were exploring.

Feeling gratitude for whatever impulse appears and expresses itself is a good practice, especially the impulses that may be more difficult to be with. Your eyes might tear up and release grief during an exploration of letting go of physical tension or you might experience a flood of creative ideas or images for your next painting or well-up with a feeling of love for your child, your partner or your pet. Anything is possible. All is welcome!

Allow it all—recognizing that you have activated another level—and then return to the statement "I have a physical body" until it feels complete for the time being. Also know that if at any time this exercise becomes too much to bear you can stop, step out of the exercise, take a break, then move to the next part of the exercise or stop all together. Self-care is important to practice at all times.

2. Once this first part is complete then say "I have a physical body but that's not all that I am" and move on to the statement, "I have an emotional body" and tune into the emotional impulses that are here now.

This might be a bit more difficult for some people to access. I like to ask "What am I feeling in my body right now? Where am I feeling this? In my heart? My gut? My throat? Am I glad, sad, mad?" Be curious about a an agitated state or any frustration. You might feel frustrated that you can't identify any emotional impulses. That is your intellect getting in the way. Gently ask it to step back a few steps, allowing it to remain in the room, and let yourself be with what else might be here. Move on to the next level of exploration whenever it feels right to do so. Don't berate yourself or expect more from yourself than what is there in that moment.

In physical theatre we explore wheels of emotional impulse where the exploration of impulses in one emotion leads into another and so on. For example one might begin exploring an impulse for anger, which leads into sorrow then into joy, followed by a rest. Then it is repeated, dropping in deeper with each cycle. This gives more structure to your exploration, use it, if it's helpful

The theatre rule of "fake it till you make it" applies here. Allow yourself to approximate an emotion until you reach it (or not). For example, faking a cough could lead into a fake (or real) cry or a lion's roar; that leads you to fake rage. Or a gasp of your breath, eyes wide with tense body to explore fear may get you moving towards connection to emotional impulse.

> *3. When this feels complete for today then close this part of the exercise with the statement, "I have an emotional body but that's not all that I am" and move on to the next level, "I have an energy body" and tune into your energy system. This level may be harder to access than physical or emotional impulses, but see what you can do. Ask yourself, How is my energy level today? Am I tired, sluggish? Am I jittery? Is one area of my body less comfortable than another and calling me to attend to it? Become aware of our nervous system and body wiring as you explore this level. It may take you into shaking or jerky movements, flicking, popping, hiccupping. Who knows? There are no mistakes – there are no wrong answers.*

With any of these explorations you might decide to have a buddy present as a witness and support for you if needed, someone to connect with and share your findings. Also you could set a timer that marks the end of each exploration. Stop if it becomes too challenging. Take breaks if you need to. Be kind to yourself so that you feel safe at all times.

> *4. When you are complete say, "I have an energy body but that's not all that I am," and move on to the statement, 'I have a creative body...' and see where this takes you.*

In this moment, writing and thinking about this exercise, I felt an impulse to explore non-human form. If I was moving rather than writing I might have become a four-legged animal prowling in the jungle moving gracefully, feeling my strength or I might have launched into a song or started to tap dance or drum out a rhythm on my leg. Anything is possible. Creative impulses freely flow from one level to another. Welcome them all. Try not to censor yourself, which is easier said than done. We are so good at censoring ourselves we often aren't even aware we're doing it. It's an ongoing practice to stop this suppression. Be kind to yourself as you explore this newfound freedom.

> *5. When this feels complete for now say "I have a creative body but that's not all that I am." Move to the next level, "I have a spiritual body," and again explore the impulses arriving as you hold and explore this level of being. Where does it take you? Do you access through the energy of your heart (that you may have explored already in one of the earlier parts of the exercise) and take it further? Do you tune into your soul? Where do spiritual impulses live in your body? How do they feel? How do they express themselves?*

These levels are all integrated and connected. Allow a certain "coming together" of the levels in this exploration. Allow your spirit to express itself through impulses gathered from all the other levels but in service of the spirit/soul levels of you. Your creative, emotional, energetic, physical impulses collectively now serve the expression of your spirit or soul. You may find that these impulses now take on a different quality or combine in a different way. See what you find.

Does this level take you another layer deeper into your creative impulses? Try not to hold any expectations that would leave you disappointed or frustrated. If that happens know that you are in the intellect and gently try to exhale and let that go.

We need to give our intellect a rest, for that aspect of ourselves is often overworked. When the spiritual level feels complete you say, "I have a spiritual body but that's not all that I am," and move on.

You see by now that you could add a customized level of impulse here if you wish. What might that be? I have a sexual body; I have an instinctual body; I have an ethereal body; anything that comes to you at this time. Open it up to your imagination and follow the impulses that reveal themselves to you.

> 6. *Then there is the grand finale: be with the "I" that is speaking. You might sit in silence and stillness for this, or not. Be with the 'I' that knows there are these various levels of awareness with infinite impulses and expressions — the "I" that observes all levels of us but isn't any one level in particular. The whole that is greater than the sum of its parts. See if you can open to this larger, all-inclusive perspective of the self without searching for or needing any specific outcome.*
>
> *If busy-ness creeps back in, know that your overactive intellect is being called into action and try to give it a rest once again. Let it know it does such a good job for you keeping you so smart and safe and liked by others but that you don't need its help right now; it can rest its weary head for another moment or two before you pick it up again. And return to the I state, the overseer of all that is You and transcends all parts or levels of the self and their impulses.*
>
> *You may find stillness and peace here or you may get even busier than you've been. Allow for any response. there's no wrong response.*

What did you discover by doing this? It's never the same twice and never the same from one person to the next. It's an exciting journey for those engaged in it.

This could become a weekly practice for you or taken in parts as a daily practice that rotates through the levels at a pace that suits you. This world of impulse is a rich and fertile field and it's waiting for you, so dip your toe in or go for a dive and swim to your heart's content.

Chapter 2

Creativity, Process vs Product

I wish I could interview my creative self to know more about what makes her tick. I know some things to be true about her. She has a mind of her own. In her world, the concepts of time and space are altered dramatically. She doesn't want to be told what to do or be controlled in any way. I suspect each creative self to be utterly unique in her wants, needs and desires.

The following piece captures a glimpse into mine. It's a conversation between the everyday self and the creative self when confronted with a challenge to create a painting specific to someone else's taste, rather than painting from my creative impulses.

The Fort MacMurray Commission—A dialogue between the artist-self (A) and her internal, creative self (C) after accepting an offer for a commissioned painting.

C: *Oh! Wow, three dentists want a ten-foot abstract painting for their waiting area and they want us to paint it...cool.*

A: *Ya, they want a triptych, painted in three separate panels that hold together but can also stand alone if the dental practice breaks up.*

C: *So ... they have to work as separate paintings ... all three of them? Hmmm ... okay, no problem.*

A: *Ya. And they have to match the upholstery and carpet in the office waiting area.*

C: *Of course they do. We can do that ... I think?*

The studio is set up. Three gallons of paint—pink, beige and blue—have been purchased and hauled home. A four by ten foot canvas is laid out and the process begins.

A: *This is good. We'll be done in no time. Cha-ching.*

C: *What are you doing? That isn't right, we need some yellow ochre right there.*

A: *Puke-yellow? Really? I don't think so. There's no yellow allowed in the palette we're using. It's pink, beige and blue only. We need to stick to the palette - so just use more pink.*

C: *I hate pink. You know that. I always have.*

A.   *Why?*

C.   *I don't know why ... maybe an angry, disowned inner female-child reflecting her gender limitations or something. I don't know, nor do I care. I just hate, what I hate, OK?*

A: *Yah, well your discontent is duly noted. But this is two thousand buckaroos. Do you think you could suck it up just this once for the sake of the sale?*

C: *Just this once, huh, who are you kidding? I don't care about the fucking sale! I feel like a cheap whore in a two bit hotel and you're pimping me out. I hate you for getting us into this.*

A: *I hear you. Just keep going. Grab the Phthalo Blue ... Will you, pleeease?*

C: *Phthalo Blue? This is such bullshit and you know it. It doesn't need Phthalo Blue, it needs...Midnight Black right there. Three vertical bars. (She slashes through the air three times violently.) That's what this sucker needs!*

A: *No! We can't put black vertical bars in this piece. It's not what they want.*

C: *Ya well I hate you for getting us into this. It's the worst thing I've ever had to do! I won't cooperate until and unless you let me add yellow ochre.*

A: *OK. OK. Calm down. Let's put it in and we'll cover it up later, under a layer of pink. There, are you satisfied?*

C: *Far from it sister, it still needs black vertical bars ... maybe just one.*

A: *No, no bars. No black anything, no straight lines. This is all pink curves with blue swirls. I tell you what. After this is done, you can paint all the black, vertical bars you want. Just help me get through this one painting and I promise you I'll never accept another commission for as long as we live. OK?*

C: DEAL.

A few days later ...

A: They loved it! It's just what they wanted. Woo hoo! We made it. I'm so pleased.

C: Well, I'm glad someone's pleased. Hand me the black paint and the 6" paint scraper, will ya?

Six large paintings with thick, vertical black bars were painted in the following weeks purging the pent up emotion in the creative self from having to adhere to strict guidelines for the commission. In order to unwind the tensions and re-balance the system, the creative self needed to be allowed to paint as she pleased, free of external or internal control. An ongoing negotiation between internal parts was played out in this exchange making it glaringly visible. If we can identify and appreciate all internal parts, their needs and desires, even unique characteristics, we can better orchestrate a harmony within.

Chapter 2 Product vs. Process

Of The Inner Parts

What internal parts are you able to identify? Write a short paragraph from each part emphasizing their unique voice. Can you locate an overseer of all the parts like the conductor of an orchestra? Write from that perspective. If you could turn into your inner creative self right now, what would she have to say?

In pairs, one partner asks a repeating question of the other, "How does your creative self express herself?" The enquirer listens to the response and records it in a notebook or on a phone. When the answer is complete, the enquirer thanks the respondent and asks the question once again. This continues for 10 minutes. The answers are then given back to the respondent for reflection. The roles are then reversed.

The creative self wants to be absolutely free, untethered and not care what others think or feel or believe about her or the value of what she has created. The creative self wants to do only what is authentic to her, following impulses and creating from her internal guide and not from forces outside of herself.

It all comes down to following impulses that are true to you and *only* you in the moment of NOW. That's it.

We can get through our entire lives without experiencing much of this present-moment, process-focused versus product-focused exploration. Practise in meditation, movement or improvisation cultivates these present state moments out of which expression and impulse are free to arise.

Once the intellect takes over and focuses on the end product we lose, big time. It's the difference between flying over the Camino de Santiago and walking it. We are robbed of the riches we so deserve. Once our head gets in the way and tries to drive towards an end result—worrying about how good it is; *"Will people like it? Will it sell? How fast can I get this done?"*—we're robbed of the gold it offers.

If we're too hung up on the end result we limit what we can be/do. We must take the cap off and allow any and all impulses to play freely in the moment. Then magic can occur

43

...or not. That needs to be OK too. The result may be something magical or something messy. It doesn't make any difference in terms of the process. The creative self has as much fun creating messes as masterpieces. The messes are the necessary steps towards the masterpiece.

Another part of the self wants winners, recognition and sales. Another part has a deep need to be seen, heard, understood, liked—that feels good to her. Staying connected to creative impulse is critical in developing one's own style, voice, presence.

Many artists have tried to earn a living from their creative work too soon and killed their creative drive. It's like asking a toddler to go out and earn a living for the family. It's not fair and sends the wrong message. Artists often have day jobs that provide income for their basic needs while supporting their passions on the side, allowing their artistic voices to mature.

There is a saying or maybe two, which I remind myself of repeatedly: *'It's only paint and paper and I have more of both.'* As I work, the other thing I remind myself of is, *'If I get one painting that I like out of ten that I make, then I'm satisfied.'* The rest can be thrown out, or be painted over creating texture for the next one, or torn up and collaged into another piece. These reminders allow me to fail, to make big mistakes and to wreck paintings while trying something new. The most exciting painting for me is always the one in process or the next to come.

When creating from a space of impulse one must not become too attached to the outcome or the product. Once the work is complete then we can step back and relate to it from a separate mind, deciding whether it goes into an exhibition, gets reworked or lines the garbage bin. We are never the best judges of whether a painting we've done is "good" so don't rush it to the bin. Live with it for a while.

Paintings may take seconds or years to complete. Some of the best paintings may be ones that we don't like initially. We aren't the best judges of our own work so why not suspend judgment and be as true to impulse in the moment as possible? There will be time to evaluated it later on. Ever met someone that you liked instantly then with further contact decided not so much? Or met someone who initially grated on you that you eventually liked? It's a bit like that with our own creations. We bring a whole host of feelings and sensations to each of them and best to not take it too seriously until we have more time and exposure to them.

When a painting is first completed, I can't see it. There seems to be no separation between the painting and myself. Over time, it gradually separates from me. I leave it and return at a later time and look at it and I see it through new eyes. Then someone else sees it and comments on it and it moves further away. Gradually it takes on a life of its own. Then I give it a title, hang it in a show where it may get purchased and taken to a new home. The separation is complete. It stands alone.

When I get to revisit paintings that I have sold in the homes where they live it's often an unusual experience that catches me off guard. Part of me knows that painting on the wall is one of mine, while another part is discovering it anew.

I once walked into one of those homes, met one of my large canvases hanging in the entranceway and taken by surprise exclaimed, *"I painted that!"*

My friend laughed out loud and replied, *"I know!"*

That particular painting was an unusual departure from what I was painting at that time and even to this day, I wonder where I was internally when I painted that piece of art. More importantly, I wonder how do I get back to that internal place so that I can paint more like it? ...maybe a series? But I'm not sure how to get back there. I could fake it and do an imitation version, but it would be glaringly visible to me that it was a copy and not an authentic impulse-driven piece or, to paraphrase Cy Twombly, an American painter from the mid 1900s, "it would be an idea-driven piece and not an image that is discovered in its primordial form."

Product vs. process is the difference between a left-brain thinking function that originates in the intellect, versus a right brain, intuitive function that resides in the body.

The left-brain, thinking function often focuses on an end product that is previously conceived, with the route to get there already mapped out. Whereas the right brain, intuitive function is in the present, experimenting and exploring with curiosity and open to going where the piece takes you. This process is more focussed on the exploration than the end result. It welcomes surprises or 'happy accidents' as I refer to them. It ends when the body says it's done. The left brain thinking approach tends to be more rigid and limiting while the right brain approach is more fluid and free.

Of course after a long time working in process there are preferences and experiences that lead one to spontaneous visual choices that produce certain effects that have pleased one in the past so even process becomes informed by preferences. Then one has to give up the familiar when a moment offers an unfamiliar, possibly more risky option that may take you into foreign territory. But to stay vital and alive one must venture into the unknown, into the forest without the compass, map, and flashlight to meet the unfamiliar where creation occurs.

46

I remember the moment and person who asked to buy my first painting ever sold. It was an unusual feeling—very unfamiliar. Part of me loves to sell my work as an artist. It feels good to be acknowledge at that creative level. A fellow painter once told me, *"We paint who we are."* When people purchase a piece of our art and hang it in their home, the artist-self receives validation and visibility. For someone who grew up not feeling seen, this moment is most significant.

Growing up, I often felt I was watering myself down or abandoning my self in order to accommodate others for love and acceptance. I was playing to my audience, be it family, friends, teachers, bosses, you name it. Give them what you think they want or end up alone and lonely. Which is what I felt anyway when I abandoned myself.

Brené Brown says, "You either walk inside your story and own it or you stand outside your story and hustle for your worthiness."

I hustled for my worthiness for many years. Once I was being seen and complimented on my creative work I would say, "Thank-you" then try to take it in. I could feel how it got blocked somewhere inside near the surface and wouldn't go past a certain point. It didn't compute on some deeper level. I wasn't able to receive it fully.

I could identify the dead zone that would take time and patience to awaken by dissolving the emotions and limiting beliefs that blocked my entry. I needed to build from scratch a new structure that could house my new reality. One where I was being seen, had value and something to say that others were interested in. My inner map was being redrawn and it was leading me home to the self.

47

Process and Physicality

I'm noticing as I write this my upper leg muscles are locked, tense and burning, especially down the outer sides. I pause, actively bend my knees and relax the vice grip that is happening largely outside of my awareness blinders. I'm wondering, why there? I have no use for those particular muscles to be working overtime in this particular moment. Maybe if I were hiking up a steep incline on a hike perhaps, but not as I'm writing.

Now as I actively relax them, having to watch them out of the corner of my awareness, steadily they release rather hesitantly. At the same time, my writing slows down substantially ... I'm feeling sluggish now.

Is my writing speed dependent upon the level of grip in my thighs? Will I stop altogether if they no longer contract? Questions I don't have answers for.

All I know is that a relaxed body while writing or painting feels impossible. I have found regular breaks in the creative activity to breathe, stretch and unwind is necessary.

I was invited to perform live as a painter at the Lula Lounge in Toronto, along with two storytellers and three jazz musicians. The storyteller, who knew me as a mover, asked me to stand still—not move too much—for fear of stealing focus. I was creating a 5X3 foot abstract painting while listening and responding to the story and music. The focus was already on me without any movement on my part added. I recall how difficult it was to be actively suppressing my physical, creative impulses to move while allowing the necessary motions needed to create the painting.

Suppress no impulses as you explore the following exercises. Use them as jumping-off points into whatever shows up from whatever level it arrives. Always keep your physical, emotional and spiritual safety in mind, so there are no negative experiences linked with opening up and revealing yourself creatively.

Exercises that gently nudge us into the present moment, listening and responding to new information without controlling the outcome, take us into Process versus Product focus.

Surrendering Weight

1. Stand facing a partner. One person is passive while the other takes the weight of the passive person's arm and moves it slow around. The person being moved is asked to stay in the moment; otherwise, they will actively take over. Giving up control and allowing one's arm to be moved without doing anything in response is challenging. It becomes easier the more you do it.

1a. Have the passive partner stand with one hand against a wall for balance and stability. Shift the body weight to one leg allowing the other leg to be lifted by your partner. As above, the person being moved tries to relax and let the mover take over the weight and manipulation of their leg.

1b. Move to the head for a greater challenge. Stand facing your partner. The passive partner bends their head forwards and places it in the hands of the mover, giving that person the full weight of their head. A hand placed on the forehead and behind the head is best for this exercise. The passive partner slowly moves to-

wards the floor until they are lying on their back, the whole time giving the weight of their head over to their partners hands.

Rest for a moment and then repeat the exercise in reverse, coming back up to standing. If the passive partner senses that they have taken the weight of the head back from the moving partner, pause and drop the head again. The holding partner might also be the first to notice this, and may give a little reminder to release the weight, through a small movement to loosen the holding pattern of the head.

Lying down, Hand Lead in 3s

2. With a partner or in a group of three have one person lay on their back, on the floor, with eyes closed beside or between the other one or two who are sitting with eyes open. The middle person's hand is placed on the top of one person's hand, palm facing downward and is led through space by the sitting person's movements of their hand. Try to break up predictable patterns of movement offering changes in direction, especially if it feels as though the person being led is taking over the lead.

Begin this exercise with one person then add a second person guiding the other hand in a different pattern of movement. The challenge is for the person lying down to allow two separate hand movements to be led through different movement patterns simultaneously. In larger groups, we've added another person on the head gently moving and loosening the head and others, one on each leg, moving them separately. It's discombobulating in all the best ways, leaving you in the present moment responding to the various stimuli.

50

Hand over Hand Lead Through Space

3. This exercise is done standing. Person A places their hand over their partner's hand, palms down. Person A then allows themselves to be led by partner B's hand around the room on an adventure. Surprise changes in direction, levels (high, medium and lower) and speeds (but you don't want to go so fast you lose your partner). Try with eyes open then eyes closed. If part of a larger group, interacting with other pairs is possible. Then switch over to the other person leading and the opposite hands used. This can also be a rotating lead if a couple of participants are without a partner and moving through the space they can pick up a loose hand from underneath one of the other partners. This then automatically splits that group and a new group is formed with another person moving freely through the space in search of a hand. Remember the lower hand always leads the action.

The Telescope - Multi-Modal Exercise Movement, Art, Writing, Theatre

1. Make a fist with your hand and hold it up to your eye so that you see through the tiny camera lens as you explore the room. Have a pad of paper and pencil (or pastel or charcoal) with you and when you see something interesting to the eye, pause and do a 10 second sketch of it and carry on. Give yourself 10-15 minutes doing this then look back over your drawings. See what shapes and textures interest you. Look at them through the camera lens of your hand and find what most interests you and mark them using another colour on the page itself. The camera lens eliminates information and focuses us on what interests us most.

> *Take your findings and combine them in a few additional drawings or take them into paintings. You could also move them or sound them or have others move and sound what they see in them or have others free associate to them with words or images that come to mind as they sit with them. Then these words become fodder for a poem or narrative that flows into movement or may be built into a theatrical piece with character work and storytelling.*

The sky's the limit when it comes to process and creativity. Always end in gratitude for the self that took you on this fertile, creative journey and respect the parts of the self that may have needed to stop. Let it be enough until the time feels right to dive back in.

Chapter 3

Creativity and Blocks

What are Blocks? What is their purpose?

I define a creative block as something that often appears 'out of the blue' without warning or explanation and interrupts our momentum during a creative activity. It can be very crafty in its ability to distract us from our current path. Its task is to manage a possible state of overwhelm that we may be approaching and which feels uncomfortable or threatening in some way.

That uncomfortable state is often anxiety- or fear-related but doesn't have to be. Not everyone carries trauma in their body. It could also be excitement or even pleasure that feels 'too hot to handle.' We get hungry, sleepy, think of things that we must accomplish right now before doing the creative activity that is right before us. Joseph Campbell's quote, "The cave you fear to enter holds the treasure you seek," works well here. However, I would expand on the word 'fear' to be any sensation that activates a level of energy or emotion in the body that feels too unfamiliar, uncomfortable or just too much.

Past traumatic experiences create hidden parts that contain emotion that the artist goes searching for, consciously or unconsciously, meeting the self along the way. Anxiety (already stored in the body or activated by creative endeavours) can lead to internal blocks to the creative process. But since we can feel more alive through creativity than we do through any other activity, learning to move through our blocks to creative flow is well worth tackling.

Our blocks are examples of the absolute best of our creativity in action. Blocks are designed to keep us safe and comfortable. They are there to protect the vulnerable parts of the self, hidden within us. Consequently, they hold great creative potential within them. These blocks are gold mines full of creative potential just waiting to be discovered.

When we are sailing along free and unchallenged, blocks aren't necessary. But the kind of art-making I'm referring to in this book can be challenging (which explains the avoidance and blocking patterns we often get into around doing it regularly). When we are creating we are engaged with forces that take us outside of our comfort zone. When we touch core material, we activate our protectors and blocks fly up like the spike strips on a highway put there by the police to stop runaway offenders.

Retrieving the Exiled parts

Our 'exiles' as Richard Schwartz defines them in *Internal Family Systems* Therapy (IFS) are parts of the self that hold our intolerable experiences. They live separated from us in a long-term storage unit we've created within the self. Among other feelings, they may hold vulnerability, fear, anger or sorrow. Many are buried so deeply in the body and mind we aren't usually aware of them on a conscious level. It's sad to think that we have these orphaned parts living inside of us that are separated from our every day self. Creatively we have assigned these parts the task of holding those unbearable experiences 'over there' so that we can get on with our lives 'over here.' They allow us to create, be in relationships, work, and live a so-called 'normal' life. These exiles carry the parts of us that we can't bear to know or feel. It really is quite miraculous when you think about it. The height of creative mastery. This process is our inner Rembrandt hard at work in service of the greater good.

Creativity can stir up material that we find difficult to hold. We then react to these uncomfortable moments by distracting ourselves away from the frightening or painful feelings. If we don't have a way to hold or process these intense feelings we block them from surfacing. This moves us away from discomfort in the moment but also prevents us from moving forwards creatively.

A variety of impulses can arise from the intelligence stored within a creative block. It may appear as a thought, a body sensation or as a feeling. One can get overactive and fidgety, or heavy and lethargic—whatever takes the focus off of the intensity that is being perceived as a threat.

Once we feel blocked or distracted we might quickly switch to a secondary level of awareness that starts to comment on or reflect back on the blocked self with negative self-talk such as, "I can't do it. It's too hard. I'm not good enough. Why even try?"

We are the creators of the block and the commentator about the block as well. We have stopped the train by putting on the brakes, but we are also the engineer that reprimands us for the action, as well as all the customers who complain about time delays and inconvenience. The block has fulfilled its purpose by distracting and sowing chaos on many levels. It has prevented us from going deeper into the unknown swamp of hungry alligators which is our inner world. Consequently, the creative block has succeeded. It's done its job.

On the other hand, many of us have an innate desire to know the whole self and live fully integrated lives. This drives our curiosity to discover and get to know these parts, so they can be freed from their burdens and living in the world with us.

In my own creative life, I've had times when feelings and sensations became so intense that it felt like I might burst into flames or explode into a thousand tiny particles. I have heard therapy clients use similar metaphors to describe their own creative experiences. If we are to engage with these powerful, energetic, emotional and spiritual forces in our creative lives, we must learn to house the intense energies that we may encounter along the way just as a house must have the correct electrical system if it is to run large appliances or the result is a fire. We need to build our nervous systems and emotional capacity to run the immense energy of a fully engaged creative life, or we run the risk of imploding or burning out.

How do we build that strength and resilience? We begin by learning about the complex inner workings of our particular patterns of resistance while inviting and leaning into the curiosity to know more. You're already on the path to a more powerful self by reading this book.

We need to build up a tolerance for what shows up and be able to hold whatever does with compassion. The attitudes, thoughts, beliefs and emotions that we have in relation to the block will strongly affect our experience of it and its impact on our creative activities.

Creative Blocks – What, How, Where and Why

There are blocks to our creativity but there is also creativity within our blocks. They can appear as intellectual thoughts, physical sensations, emotional states or spiritual experiences. Let's start by addressing the emotional blocks to creativity, as they are some of the more difficult ones to identify and get a handle on.

There are three parts to an emotional block - the raw material, the guards or protectors, and the attitudes towards these protectors and core material. Richard Schwartz has developed a method of therapy that informs this discussion. I have studied this therapy model but I am not a certified IFS practitioner so may not hold its theories in their purest form. I draw from it as one reference point of many.

Our blocks attempt to keep the every day self away from stored thoughts, feelings and sensations caused by past, uncomfortable or traumatic events in order to avoid any further pain or suffering. Blocks are protecting us from any further injury. They are often highly skilled and demonstrate some of the best of our creative energy.

Animals protect and defend themselves in a variety of creative ways. A mother bird draws the attention of a predator away from her nest by feigning a broken wing while squawking and dancing about. Our blocks do something similar; in creative ways they trick us over and over again in order to draw attention away from the raw, intolerable, uncomfortable feelings.

Then there are mental attitudes or thoughts, beliefs and feelings we have towards the blocks themselves. These secondary attitudes may not even be aware of the raw material or the real function of the block (one of guarding or protection). The mental comments or attitudes can be incessant - I call them the "chatter from the peanut gallery".

Much of our creativity is dedicated to keeping us distracted from our raw material, but we are unaware of this. Our secondary attitudes further distract us with judgmental thoughts such as, 'What a loser. You'll never be creative. You're not that good. You'll never be an artist. Mary is so much better. Just give it up and walk away. Take up knitting or better yet, read a book. I think I'm hungry. Do we have any doughnuts in the house?' Our creativity and genius has shifted to distraction rather than embarking on a deeper dive into our selves through our art.

A creative block can also appear on an intellectual level in the form of boredom. I'm always suspicious of this culprit when it shows up. There will almost certainly be suppression of impulses happening simultaneously at another level. There is nothing boring about us or our creative activities, so if you notice that you're feeling bored, look for a block that has been activated.

Not Good or Bad, Better or Worse – Just Interesting

We make judgments about what is and isn't good; we then accept what we think is good and reject what we think is bad. But whether our creativity is flowing and we are producing artistic results that we like, or whether we're blocked, feeling frustrated, lost and confused, it is only a problem when we favour one state over the other. Both positions hold infinite creative possibilities. It comes down to whether we can sit quietly and wait or explore the block on its own terms with an open, curious mind or fall into patterns of thought and feelings that cause us to shut down and move away from the moment. If we sit still and turn towards the block with an open mind, then blocks may prove to be even more interesting than being on a creative roll.

Who's to say that the breakthrough self is any more desirable or interesting than the blocked self? Only you.

If I welcome the blocked moments, become curious towards the impulses within it I can explore them creatively by moving, painting, sounding, writing, expressing the physical, emotional, intellectual nuances of the block. I may then find this exploration as interesting or even more interesting than the states where there is freedom and flow. When I encounter a block I know that I am getting close to the cave where the vulnerable, core material resides. I get excited and intrigued, wanting to know more, explore more, discover more.

In the flow we are often in a more comfortable, familiar place than we are when we're feeling blocked. To link a block with the possibility of richer, deeper discoveries and be able to sit with our attention to the moment, strategically situates us on the edge of creation.

Creative blocks deserve the same open curiosity and respect that we give our breakthroughs and victories ...they are important messengers and chock-a-block full of creative genius. It's time they got our full attention and their fair share of the glory.

Changing our Relationship to Our Blocks

What is your relationship to your blocks? Is it a healthy, open, loving relationship or a controlling, tight, mastery-over approach? If it's the latter likely you will lose. I have learned, as a therapist, trying to muscle through a block doesn't work. We have developed these defences to protect us and they are very good at it. They will out maneuver us every time. They are our creative genius working at the highest level with the purest intention to protect us. We won't be able to topple the protectors. To attempt to do so will only strengthen their resolve. If we try to tear them down they will arise with more force to perform the job they were assigned to do; defend and protect us.

Our relationship to our blocks is no different than an external relationship in that way. Arguing with someone, shouting at them, putting them down or storming away in a huff versus sitting and listening trying to understand them with an open heart results in very different outcomes, as we all know.

Blocks need to be honoured, respected, given their due and be thanked for the vital job they do: keeping us safe and out of harm's way. Good job, I say. At times, they overwork on our behalf and we need to re-educate them, reassure them we are safe and thank them for being with us and for the great job they are doing.

If we try to skip over or ignore and muscle through, we miss the guidance offered in the moment. That might be to slow down and feel, to bring connection and awareness to the moment, be curious. We need to bring play to the moment and explore the block in whatever way we can through movement, sound, visual art, theatre or writing.

In the following exercises we explore a a variety of ways to approach blocks, but first you need to work on your inner attitude towards your blocks. First you must stop wanting your blocks to go away or attacking them with a barrage of negative, critical thoughts and beliefs. Instead, start being open to what blocks have to offer, grateful for their protection and thankful to them for all their hard work.

It's time to build a strong, healthy relationship with our creative selves and the first step to that is addressing our fears and blocks with the respect that they deserve.

Moving Through Blocks

Resistance often rises up just before a breakthrough so the anticipation of a creative breakthrough can become linked when encountering a block. It is similar to meeting a block when meditating. One hangs out doing nothing with it until something shifts. I call it "hanging out in the neighbourhood,"—a time when we may not know exactly where we are going but we hang out in the general vicinity until something reveals itself.

Dissolving a creative block might be as simple as slowing down and being curious as to what is happening at that moment. If we know that we activate inner protectors when we feel a threat as we touch our raw material, then we could breathe and calm ourselves. We could stay with the fear or the discomfort and possibly break through the block into a deeper creative process.

Simply accepting the block and what it reveals is valuable.

A friend and teacher of mine once said, *"We need to love those messy little poems; they are the stepping stones to inspired works to come."* I apply that statement to all creative endeavours. Lift out the word 'poems' and replace it with any art form. Instead of judging and rejecting them, we must love those messy little paintings, drawings, movements, stories, scenes, songs, sounds or other works, and value them as much as we do any other creative outcome. If we can do that, then we're home free and, surprisingly, our blocks dissolve. We come to understand we're not fighting them any longer. We listen to what they have to say and acknowledging their value. Then, working with them, we find a way forward.

Alternatively, accepting the block for a defined period of time might also be helpful. The block might turn out to be the fallow field that is re-mineralizing by lying still and less active than when it is bursting with growth. One state is as important as the other—and equally as interesting—if you are able to maintain your equanimity and an open heart towards both states. In the exercises at the end of this chapter, I offer you some techniques for bringing your creativity and curiosity to your blocks to engage with them, finding ways to be as energized by those blocked parts of yourself as you are when your creativity is flowing.

Blocks hold an infinite amount of creative potential. Blocks have provided the fodder for many a creative moment. People have written plays and built full performances from them. An acting student once wrote a one-woman show about her addiction to alcohol and how it held her back from being the performer that she knew she could be. It was full of humour and humanity and she allowed herself be be seen as both vulnerable and strong. She was able to recognize her inner saboteur and give it a voice to speak it's truth. She wrote a very successful play that transformed her life from one where her addiction was running the show to one where her empowered performer was in the spotlight. She was able to follow her dreams at long last.

Ask yourself: *"Am I close to a breakthrough, feeling scared and deploying the guards to distract me off the trail to a more creative life?"* If you can ask the question you will likely get an honest answer. Then you know where you stand. You might be able to negotiate with the guards, reassuring them that you're aware of them, thanking them for their protection. Let them know you're safe and then you may be able to move through the block.

Asking yourself what level the block is showing up on is a good starting point.

"Am I feeling blocked intellectually and need new stimulation or ideas or input to work from?

"Am I feeling blocked emotionally and need to stop and breathe and connect with what I'm feeling or get some help from a therapist?"

"Am I feeling isolated and lonely and need a friend to talk with, share my process, feelings or struggles for support?"

Admitting to a friend that you are blocked goes a long way towards releasing any shame that you might be carrying. Being curious and non-judgmental towards whatever is showing up is critical to keeping the creative channel open and flowing.

Taking a short break or a walk outdoors might free up some energy. Breathing with hands on your chest and belly while checking in with what's going on inside might be just the right thing to do.

Writing or painting or moving the block can be fruitful for the artist. How does your block express itself? I've seen visual artists with journals displayed in the gallery filled with pages of one, lone mark repeated over and over in a meditative way. Maybe a tantrum punching pillows is in order.

Ushio Shinohara, a Japanese artist, paints with boxing gloves dipped in paint punching the canvas. That's creative. Let the block have centre stage and express itself just as you would offer to a friend. You'd enquire what was happening for them and offer your support.

Taking a slightly different direction, changing it up may free up your energy and get it flowing again. In art making, a change of colour or a shift from brushes to scrapers or adding an element of collage may do the trick. You need to know yourself and know how this protector works and what might re-engage your connection to the moment.

Sometimes we need the input of a teacher or outside person to boost our ideas or energy. We may write, draw or move together with others. Feedback and sharing can go a long way to revitalizing our passion and enthusiasm for our art making. It can be an arduous and lonely path at times. Recognizing when one needs to reach out and add fresh input is critical. Finding connection and support from others can be a lifeline for an artist.

If you're feeling blocked creatively or emotionally, find physical body movements that reflect this inner state. Curling and stretching, breathing in and out may help shift the block. Lie down and run through your body tensing, then releasing different parts; ankles, feet, legs, hands, arms belly, torso, shoulders face, finally the whole body to get more energy flowing to help shift the block.

Lean into what is here now, amplify it and explore it. Write it, paint it, move it, sound it, express it in whatever way you can. Welcome it as best you can and accept your current limits.

See if you can recognize your hesitance—even welcome it, thank it for the hard work its doing to keep you safe. Tell it right here, right now you're safe. Ask it to step back and give you room to explore—it can even stay in the room or guard the door. Place a pillow in the corner so it can sit comfortably. Thank it for its excellent work. Then explore these following exercises knowing you have a safety guardian in the room.

Chapter 3 Exploring Your Blocks

Welcoming Emotion - A Multi-Modal Approach

A block likely has emotional content in it that we are resisting so simply asking "What am I feeling right now - am I angry, sad, scared?" might be a starting point for your curiosity. If you have trouble identifying the emotion, you could experiment with possibilities. As I've mentioned already, in theatre we say "Fake it till you make it."

Fake an angry rant or a sorrowful cry or hide fearfully under a blanket, then write about your experience. Move it, sound it, paint it, creatively associate with it, listen to music that expresses a certain mood for you. For instance, I find Josh Groban's song "To Where You Are," helps to unlock my sorrow.

Be curious and invitational to all that's there. Say, "Tell me more. I want to know more about that, please."

Be receptive. Sit in an open, invitational position in the body, palms open facing up, and breathe into your heart and surrender to what is asking to be known. Open up and be receptive to all that arrives. Use your creativity to express what's there.

Physical

Wants, Needs, Desire — A Multi-Modal Inquiry

1. It's amazing what a body position can do for us. Curl your body into a tense ball, then gradually unfold until you are in an open body position with arms reaching out and up inviting in whatever is here.

2. Just slump over and collapse for a moment then reach up and out through your spine and arms. Feel the difference. You're mood will shift from one position to the other.

3. If there is something that you want in your life write it on a piece of paper or find an object that represents it and stand across the room from it and see what happens as you move towards it. Your relationship to it is revealed - your thoughts, beliefs, feelings and sensations in relationship to having that thing which you so dearly want but can't reach becomes clear.

Allow any writing, drawing, movement or feelings to be expressed as you do this. Give yourself time. Take breaks if you need to. Worlds will reveal themselves. Record and engage with this process. It's the grit that creates a pearl in the oyster, the inner creative process inviting you to go deeper.

The inner judges and critics that chatter constantly at us from inside our minds are also there to keep us safe. They are aspects of our creativity in action. Have you noticed they lack compassion? Much of what they hurl at us we would never dream of saying to another person, nor would we get away with it. Yet we seem to give parts of ourselves permission to trash other parts vehemently, when no one else is watching.

I did a skit once where my forearm was inside a shoe box and once the lid was off my hand became a wild thing that was trying to strangle me. My other hand was busy holding it at bay, protecting me. This skit displayed, in physical form, the parts of the self that have our best interests in mind and parts that are out to get us. This is a rich playing field for creative drama and movement.

Clowns love these rogue body parts that are at odds with other parts of the self.

Rogue Body Parts

Choose a body part that takes on a mind of its own and turns on the self. Perhaps a foot that decides to walk in another direction or a hand that takes over the drawing and becomes possessed by a rogue spirit. It is necessary to keep in mind your physical safety while doing this but surprises will appear that can lead to some interesting writing, movement and theatrical results.

Drum Dialogue

1. How does the protector/defender play physically? Stand facing a partner, with two hand drums and beaters, drums in front of the body. Beat the drum you are holding listening and interacting in sound with your opponent doing the same. Move around the room talking with each other through the drums. Defend yourself with your sound while challenging your opponent. When the time is right attempt to hit the other person's drum with your beater. This is the winning move or you may want to go to best of three. The tension builds as you go. Feel the fierce protector through the drum.

Always keep physically safe with these exercises. Celebrate your win at protecting your drum. Then write about it or draw it or find a movement sequence that depicts the story of it and share with others. Where else in life have you had to defend yourself from others? When have you succeeded and when did you not?

Interviewing the Protector

Sit facing a partner. One person, in the role of interviewer, asks the other for permission to speak to the protector or defender. It may sound something like this, "May I speak to the one who protects?"

The other replies, "Yes I am the protector. You may speak to me."

The first person asks, "What is your job?"

The other answers, "My job is to protect."

Now there is an established voice to dialogue with and the person questioning asks the repeating question, "As protector, how do you defend?"

Wait for the answer and record it for the person answering. Then say "Thank you" and repeat the question again, "How do you defend?" Listen, record and repeat the question. Continue for a set period of time, 5-7 minutes is a good length. Then share experiences and reverse roles.

Look at your responses and write from what stands out for you, taking it deeper.

Protecting the Vulnerable

Find physical postures for the protector. Have a pile of foam balls that wouldn't hurt a flea when thrown at anything, and pelt someone as they defend themselves with raised arms. Find your fearless warrior/defender. Have another person be the vulnerable soul that hides behind you as you defend and protect against the at-

70

tack from the foam balls. Growl and sound out the defender.

Get onto all fours and find the animal bodies and sounds of the protector/defender. Be the threatened animal poised to attack the predator. Maybe it's the dragon or lion at the mouth of the cave protecting her babies. Play in this energy exploring sound and movement. Then write or draw from your experiences. Share your findings verbally or visually or dramatically through movement.

Balance, Fall and Recovery

What dramatic scenario could you find yourself in where one part of the self is risking danger and another is protecting or defending her? This can be played with physically with balances, fall and recovery. Standing on your feet lean forwards and linger at the point of imbalance. Tilt further until you fall off balance and then recover your balance. Try it in another direction; forwards, sideways, backward. Keep your knees slightly bent. Have a partner supporting your weight as you lean off balance then slowly return to balance. Be open to experiencing all the feelings and sensations that arrive with this. Write, draw and share these findings with a partner and the group.

The Rant

Allow yourself to be a very critical, judgmental person. Focus your attention on some imaginary enemy somewhere in the room, but not directly at anyone around you. Everyone in the room will be speaking all at once. Blast that enemy like a person with nothing to lose and no filters. In Big Mind, a practice based on *principles drawn from Voice Dialogue and Zen Bud-dhism, developed by Genpo Roshi, there was a voice called 'the voice of the f*cked up self.' Find that voice and go on a rant. Then pause and write it up, what was said and the feelings it stirred. It may trigger shame or fear. Create a container that holds this volatile energy; set a timer, have an observer holding the space, share with others, ground yourself at the end and reconnect with the grounded, calm self. Don't drive any heavy equipment for at least an hour. (That's a joke with an element of truth to it.)*

The Troll and the Lamb

The physicality of the critic is twisted and gnarled, tightly bound and tense. It may be troll-like. Find your inner troll that lives under the bridge and have the in-nocent little lambs crossing over top, unsuspecting of the negativity and danger. We all have innocent little lamb parts and twisted troll parts inside of us. What do yours look like? What are they saying towards them-selves and towards others?

Write the troll and lamb scripts both as monologues and dialogues. In groups of two, share your writing. Dramatize parts with your partner feeding you the lines. Costume accessories and props (scarves, hats, etc.) may be chosen to add a creative element to the play. Embody the critic leaning into it fully, finding the contrasting elements to the innocence of the lamb.

There are no bad parts. The twisted, gnarled parts are delightfully nasty in their thoughts and actions and have undiscovered riches. Start mining your gold! Get out pastels or paint and capture the adventure in colour and form, then move the shapes and forms in

72

the drawing. By now you are surely getting the feel of the interconnection and flow that is possible from one art form to another. Where you jump into the river from has many, many options ...but it's the same river.

Visual Art

Tight Drawing

1. If you're feeling tight, grab some paper and a pastel and draw a "tight" drawing. Keep going until it begins to loosen up. If you're feeling angry, try painting or scraping a thick, red zigzag line (old credit cards work well for this) on the canvas or choose your preferred colours and tools. Growl like an angry dog, then write a monologue for the dog telling its story of how it's feeling, how it got here and what it needs.

Meandering Line

2. If you feel lost, take an oil pastel or charcoal and allow it meander over the surface as a line that is lost and doesn't know where it is going. Pause and write words on the page; if creative associations, songs, images, etc. arise, write them down then continue. Place a stone, or any object you choose, somewhere on the page and, with your line, explore the relationship between your line and the stone or object which represents the block. Explore the many ways that you might approach the stone. This could also be a red "X" placed on the page where you choose. Then play with lost-to-found by drawing a meandering line that finds and discovers its destination—or not. Write about the destination you have found or the journey you've been on. It might be the Holy Grail or one of Dante's Circles of Hell. Either is valid or anything in between.

Sponge Blotting

3. If you feel frustrated blot a piece of paper with a sponge soaked with paint, maybe one in each hand, eyes open or closed, curious about what's here, now wanting to be known.

Soaked With Sadness

4. If you're sad you could soak a page of heavy watercolour paper, then drop blue or black ink onto its surface watching it flow and mix with your tears. You might howl or wail as you do this, expressing the feeling that is there. None of it has to be perfect. Remember, "Fake it till you make it." Allow yourself to stagger through the exercise like the first run through of a play, looking as "bad" as you need to. Remember this is just an exploration – let yourself explore without worrying about what others think or feel.

If worry is present, then give it a body position, movement, sound and text. This is about loosening up your flow and giving yourself permission to explore further and deeper into the unknown. That is where creativity lives...in the unknown parts of the self.

Writing

Judges Journal

Having a Judges Journal where you dump all the thoughts and vitriol that the inner judges spew is a useful practice. You will see patterns and favourite lines that your judges spout in particular situations whether it's at a party, in the art studio, with family, friends, lovers, at work or school. Getting to know the patterns of the judges is beneficial. Challenging and working with them creatively gives you a leg up on their control. Saying to them, "I know you're just trying to keep me safe and I'm grateful for that but maybe you could just step back a bit and give me a little more room for a moment. I'm sure we'll be safe doing this but if not then I welcome your protection once again."

You'll be surprised how well they respond. They are tired of being in these guarding roles to our endangered child. But they need to be worked with and not shamed or treated with anger or resentment or I guarantee you'll only get more tightly bound to them. It only reinforces the importance of the judge if it's met with confrontation. It's built to defend against criticism and aggression.

If I meet a critic or judge in the art studio, which I often do, I say, "Hey, I know you're trying to help me but what you're saying isn't helpful. If you don't have anything nice to say, don't say anything at all" or "Here's what would be helpful to hear from you." Then thank it for its cooperation.

These critical parts are there to protect us and are happy to take a break from their roles as our bodyguards so long as they know that we are safe and well looked after. Developing other parts of the self that can step in, negotiate with the judges and reassure the protectors, will help manage their levels of activation. This development allows for more creative freedom.

Be grateful and respectful for your exploring self, honour the pace and depth that feels right for you today, whether it's leaps and bounds or baby steps, let it be perfect just as it is.

Chapter 4

Creativity and Boundaries

"Daring to set boundaries is about having the courage to love ourselves, even when we risk disappointing others ... "

~Brené Brown

Boundaries are essential, yet often overlooked. The topic could fill a book of its own. I will only be touching on them here, but I recommend some significant time and attention given to exploring them if you haven't already.

Anyone who has ever struggled with addictive behaviour confronts their internal boundaries regularly. Artists often have broader, freer and more flexible boundaries which allows for experimentation into new territories of creation. A surplus of self-destructive behaviours can also accompany this freedom.

I have struggled with boundaries throughout my life, resulting from poor boundaries at home, growing up. I had parents who didn't boundary their emotional behaviours or boundary other people's behaviours towards us as children, causing lasting injuries. Also, my parents didn't teach us healthy boundaries growing up.

I don't want to get too far off the topic here. Parts of me want to charge off in a different direction right now to tell you much more about this. I must pause and breathe. With so many parts wishing to speak all at once, I'm getting a bit lost and overwhelmed. That is part of my story and one of my core challenges. You might already know this about me from reading this book and can relate to it in yourself. So let's breathe and explore this potent topic together.

We all need boundaries. If you want a creative life and healthy relationships, you need to know when to exercise boundaries and when to give them a rest. It's safe to say that we all have areas in our lives where we could strengthen our boundaries, and areas where we could ease up on the restrictions that we've placed on ourselves.

There is often a direct relationship between lax boundaries and rigid ones. Where there is a rigid boundary, there is often a slack one. Like muscles in the body, one group might be overworking and tense while another, interconnected group, is underworked and weak. This muscle imbalance in the system may make us more vulnerable to injury. A physical practise that builds balance, strength and flexibility creates a healthier body.

There was a librettist at the Banff Music Theatre Dept, a guest artist from England who shared his fear of therapy with me. He thought delving into his emotions, and past trauma would kill his creative drive. That may well have been true for him, I don't know, but a diet of coca-cola, chocolate bars and alcohol might also be harming his potential.

We need to know when to say yes to ourselves and others and when to say no. Saying no to others when it causes disappoint, anger, rejection or abandonment is difficult for many of us, especially women.

Women learn early in life to abandon their needs to care for others. This makes us good partners and mothers. Women are taught that it's more important to keep those around us happy and not consider our own happiness. We often gather resentment for this, which then blocks our creativity and undermines our relationships. We are labelled selfish and uncaring if we look after ourselves first. Men get more of a pass on this one it would seem.

In theatre, self-abandonment scenarios can be explored. We can become more comfortable with paying attention to ourselves and what we want, need and desire. Luckily we can unlearn some of these unhealthy patterns of behaviour that no longer serve us personally, creatively or socially.

In terms of personal boundaries, I've struggled with eating issues over the years. One situation stands out for me at university where I grabbed the hungry bull by the horns. I spoke firmly to a part of me that was longing for more. *"No more cake, but we can have a bubble bath with our yellow rubber duckie."* I was in a younger part of the self at the time. I hauled her off to the tub and cried for an hour, commiserating over all the woes of my past, present and bleak future.

Just being with the grief, disappointment and emptiness that I was feeling seemed to break the conflict I was in with food. It was a pivotal moment in understanding the role that food played in soothing my inner sad child. I saw the direct connection of my emptiness and sadness to my need to soothe and comfort myself with sweets. Mom baked a cake or cookies to apologize for her angry outbursts and loss of control with us as children. It was a comforting apology with a return to some sense of care and safety.

I was running that scenario in my own adult life. I was soothing the scared, unloved empty parts of myself with food—or trying to, rather unsuccessfully. I came to realize that food couldn't meet the emotional needs of the self where she longed to be met. Over-eating worsened my predicament adding guilt, self-loathing and a sense of failure to the original pain and suffering.

Boundaries directly relate to our needs; safety being one of the most important of these. Needs are unique to each individual. Trying to negotiate them in a partnership requires some clarity, creativity, playfulness and humour. What seems simple can become difficult for many couples trying to find their comfort, validation and proof of being loved in the actions of another. We need to embrace our own needs before we can respect and embrace our partners. Communication and compassion go a long way in doing this successfully.

It takes curiosity and inquiry to find all the places where we could lovingly and firmly apply stronger boundaries. The same holds true for the places where we need to relax rigid boundaries. They may be there from past experiences and no longer be needed.

It is important in creative work, especially physical theatre and movement to discover one's comfort levels, the zone of exploration where one is challenged but not overwhelmed. I have had moments in my art and therapy training where I had my boundaries challenged physically, creatively, emotionally, energetically and spiritually resulting in an expanded playing field both creatively and relationally. A good teacher or therapist will help find this optimal zone, while maintaining safety and respect for who we are and what we can tolerate at the time.

Boundaries create a healthy structure for our lives. They grow and change with us so those we had in the past we may no longer need and those we didn't need in the past we may need now.

In order to give ourselves the time and space we need to create, then we need to boundary other activities that will steal that time away from us. Are you giving yourself the time and opportunity you need to be creative? If you're not, why do you think that is? What feelings come up when you sit with yourself in this place of acknowledgement right now?

Chapter 4 Exercises

Physical Boundary Inquiry - Personal Space

1. This exercise explores where our body ends and another's begins. With a partner press back to back, hands to back, shoulder to shoulder, hands to shoulders, side hip to side hip, hands to hands pressing forwards and backwards across a room exploring the physical boundaries of the body. Adding a line to it, such as, "Get out of my way," or "Back off," takes the exercise to a different level.

On all fours, connect right shoulder to left shoulder pressing forward and back or sit on the floor with feet pressing against feet to further explore body boundaries.

This physical touch may be too uncomfortable for some people, so the exercise may need to be modified.

Try placing a large bolster or pillow between bodies to make it comfortable if necessary. Emotional comfort and physical safety are important.

2. With a partner link arms at the elbow standing side by side. One pulls the other forward through the room saying, "You're coming with me." The other resists saying, "No I'm not," to express a boundary.

I recall doing this exercise with a fellow student in a practice session in psychotherapy during our training at the *Integral Healing Centre, Toronto.* We were at her home for this. Her normally very mild-mannered orange tabby cat named Lucy, took a flying leap across the room and landed on the top of my bare leg. It was summer and I was in shorts. The cat dug her claws in and slid down my leg leaving streams of bloody scratches the length of my leg. Needless to say the session was suspended for the clean-up of my wounds. The beloved pet had performed her important duty to protect her owner.

Writing

Crossing Boundaries

Write about a time in your life when a boundary of yours was crossed by someone else.

Write about a time when you crossed a boundary, either one of your own or someone else's.

What feelings arose from this writing? Share them with a partner or the group. Rewrite the scene as you would have preferred it to go - dramatize one of the written scenarios using a partner or people from the group.

Movement and Theatre

Needs and Response

Set up a dramatic scene where one partner begs, pleads, is needy, sad, distressed while the other feigns indifference and shows annoyance saying, "Go away. Stop bothering me. I don't care about you. Can't you see, I'm busy." One participant can be at a lower level while the other is at a higher level. Move around the room with one following the other begging for a dime or some food that the other has. Pause to write for 20 minutes on your findings. Share it with your partner, then switch roles.

I fell into this role as beggar to another character who was a kingly high status soul in my mask work during a theatre class. I loved playing the grovelling, lowly soul begging to be loved.

Where do these experiences take you emotionally? Is there a time in your life when you felt yourself to be in either of these roles?

Other Possible Scenarios —

Set up a scene where one person sees another's need for food or help of some kind, and tries to help but gets rejected. Reverse roles.

Set up a scene where one is in need and the other helps them in some way, maybe one fakes a fall and the other helps them up. Where the gesture is received with gratitude.

Which one of these was the most difficult for you and which was the easiest. Write about why.

Share your findings with your partner and combine them into a short story line with simple movements and minimal text to tell a story. Share it with the others.

Art

Exploring Boundaries

Draw or collage your findings on boundaries and the lack thereof, plus the emotions embedded within them using art supplies and magazine images. Share this with your partner or the group.

Chapter 5

Creativity and Trauma

A Journey through Healing, a Return to Self

How Trauma Splits Us

I recall Marion Woodman, a Jungian analyst and author, sharing a dream that she said she'd heard from a number of her therapy clients, where the dreamer goes into their cellar and sees two small black eyes peering out from a dark corner of the basement. When asked who they were and why they were hiding, they said, "I am your soul. I was hiding because if I had come out any sooner, you would have killed me."

When there has been trauma in our backgrounds and that covers most human beings to some degree, we are altered by it. I define trauma as any deeply distressing or disturbing experience that terrifies and overwhelms a person and their current resources. The after-effect may be disconnection from parts of the self, resulting in a bound state or an overactive, anxious state that won't settle. The person is often left feeling stuck, unable to move forward, frozen in time. The present and the past get lodged together.

Traumatic experiences may affect the psyche at a very early age – some pre-verbal/pre-cognitive, before language and thought develop – fracturing the sense of self. We intuitively create patterns of adaptation in response to the trauma affecting our thoughts, beliefs, emotional responses and sensations in the body. They may appear as physical, emotional, intellectual, spiritual or energetic patterns of behaviour.

These patterns are created as a means of coping with the uncomfortable, painful or frightening situations in which we live. We can be negatively interfered with in many ways – physical, emotional, spiritual or intellectual – our sense of self altered by others who are, in their own right, wounded and fractured. Abuse, physical or emotional, through interference or neglect, compromises a child's sense of safety. Then all inner systems adjust, moving the child from a relaxed state of self-exploration to a hyper-vigilant focus on the outer world. A traumatized self, full of protective patterns of behaviour is the outcome.

Developmental trauma occurs in childhood where abuse or neglect takes place over an extended period of time. For an infant, crying is a mode of expression and communication to the parent from the baby's need in the moment. "She's such a good baby, she never cries," may be a child that is adapting to a parent who can't cope with a crying baby. The baby has already sensed stress and anxiety in the parent and has shut down her emotion to accommodate a parent's needs.

Of course, sometimes she might just be a happy, contented baby. One usually sees a happy, contented parent as well in those situations.

Many adults can't cope with the sound of a crying infant because it triggers difficult feelings for them. When an adult shushes an infant too loudly or bounces and pats them too vigorously with agitation in their body, they are likely being triggered by the child's cry for help. The child, intuitive and attuned to the adult, may begin to take care of the adult's emotions soon after birth. Babies are sensitive and instinctual. They learn to smile and coo to get positive results. If crying results in a caregiver that is too threatening for the chid, then the child may alter her behaviour by shutting down emotions.

I have clients in my practice who have never been able to cry as children or adults – it wasn't an option for them. Maybe they tried it once or twice as a child and decided—not from the intellect or thinking brain, but from body instinct—that it was too dangerous for their survival, so they stopped.

If threat or isolation or suffering is all we've ever known, then it becomes the norm; we know no different state. Our patterns of adaptation go to work to make our lives tolerable by shaping our reality, possibly through fantasy or other forms of escape.

The patterns are there to protect us from present or future harm. Because these patterns were so critical to our safety and wellbeing, they remain active long after we no longer need them. They become automatic reflexes to certain stimuli; these reflexes are difficult to turn off, even when the logical brain knows better.

Growing up, I heard a story told describing a mother who said, "I just have to put a feather in the doorway of any room I want to keep Johnny out of." I didn't think anything of it at the time, but later on, I wondered what had caused the child's fear of feathers. Had the child experienced something physically painful caused by a bird or something emotionally or visually scary involving a bird? And why on earth would a mother then use a child's fear to control his behaviour? That is, at best, unconscious, insensitive action on the part of the mother.

Infants and small children are literally dependent on parents for their survival. They will override the self very quickly to protect a parent or abusive adult. This is a way of coping with feelings of terror, powerlessness, grief or isolation in the body. This protection of the adult creates a shutdown, stuck state of longing for more, but never getting it. In my experience as a therapist, many adults have this feeling state in the body to some degree.

In my practice I see patterns of thought and behaviour that have been passed down through families and generations of people, ancestral patterns that don't serve the lives of those living them out today.

For example, the lesson, "men don't cry" taught by fathers or grandfathers who repress emotions to show strength and manliness does not serve the people caught in this pattern. This teaching can create a lineage of health issues as well as emotional problems that run through the family, generation after generation.

The question, "What are you feeling in the body?" versus "What are you feeling?" accesses different inner worlds. Many people are unable to connect with either question. The questions may even bring up shame for the person being asked. The client may feel guilty and defensive that they are disconnected from the self. They feel they should hide this terrible fact. They think they should know better, be better or do better. We can be our own worst enemies. One of the first things I say to a client is, "This isn't your fault."

There is enough information and help available that we can identify, repair and integrate the lost or wounded parts of ourselves. Those parts have usually gone into hiding or become distorted or even self-destructive as a means of coping with traumatic experiences.

Dr. Richard Schwartz, tells us there are no bad parts, only ill-informed and suffering parts. These parts are expressing something from the past. Once identified and understood, the blocked emotion can be unburdened. Understanding and compassion is offered to these parts.

The self was coping with difficult situations, doing the best she could with what she knew. These younger parts don't have the maturity and self-knowledge we have as adults. We need to embrace and offer compassion to those younger selves who got us through a host of difficult times with very little help or support.

It's important to know that whatever happened to us, as infants and children, wasn't our fault—it shouldn't have happened. We didn't deserve it. Letting go of the guilt and shame or the belief that it was our fault is an essential part of the healing process. We were only children. Parents or adults were the ones responsible. We can understand that they were probably traumatized themselves, but it doesn't mean that what happened to us was right or okay. We are entitled to have all of our feelings relating to our experience of what happened.

When we witness ourselves shutting down or sending parts of ourselves into hiding, we are seeing the creative self in action. It wasn't safe to be seen, to feel or to express ourselves so we did what we needed to do—shutdown and disconnect in order to survive the situation.

Bravo. Good job. You did the right thing—the best you could have done under the circumstances. Feel grateful to the self for doing what it thought was needed at the time. Thank that part of the self for its good work towards preserving the vulnerable self.

But now, as an adult, the situation is different. It's safe to explore the cost to the self for having to perform those protective, defensive actions. You managed to get through home, school, work, and relationships carrying the compromised self with you under your wing.

Now, let's find those lost parts and get them help. Let's hear and see and experience how it was for them as they free up trapped impulses and parts—in safe ways of course. If it becomes overwhelming or "not safe" at any point during the expression, then we run the risk of re-traumatizing the self all over again. If we find the "window of tolerance" as Dr. Pat Ogden calls it, and provide resources and support to the stuck part, it is then allowed to respond energetically and emotionally in a corrective manner. The charge is released and a new relationship to the past traumatic event is formed. It is reframed and placed in the past where it belongs rather than running the present moment.

We can't change our histories, but we can change our relationship to them when we hold that history with compassion and understanding in strong, loving arms. Susan Aaron, Psychodramatic Bodywork Originator, has a message from the inner-adult self to the inner-child self;

"You didn't do anything wrong

Of course you're scared (angry, sad)

You have every right to be scared (angry, sad)

You lived in danger – but I'm here now

It's safe now

You're not in danger

You're not in danger anymore because your adult is here making it safe

I'm sorry I wasn't here then

I want to take care of you

You come into my arms whenever you're afraid and I will comfort you

That's my job now

You're perfect just the way you are and if anyone says any-thing different – they're wrong

I love you

I take care of you first

You are my first priority

And then I can do everything else that I do in the world."

———————

We don't have to be triggered by our pasts. We can live in the present. When we do get triggered, we can notice it, but not act upon it. We can then take care of ourselves in a loving way that doesn't harm or affect our current lives or relationships.

Even if the intellect can't explain or understand why certain fears are with us, the body holds the answers, and with curiosity and inquiry the origins may be discovered.

Not everyone will choose to go through a process to find out the answers. It's usually out of necessity that someone comes into psychotherapy to work with fears that are negatively affecting their day-to-day lives.

I used to describe our parts as "the Good, the Bad and the Ugly" until I learned from Dr. Schwartz that there are no bad parts—although some intentionally hurt both themselves and others from a place of fear or anger, having been so scared or hurt themselves. A wounded animal when trapped will often respond with aggression. These inner parts that are hurt or scared may act out aggressively against perceived threat in order to defend and protect. But they are not "bad."

As we peel off the layers of misinformation we've gathered over a lifetime (through statements such as "shame on you," or actions such as feathers placed in doorways), we uncover the authentic self of us: innocent, pure, loving, strong, creative, spontaneous, free-spirited.

All parts of us need love and guidance — to be embraced by a central mature, loving, core self. Our natural, uninjured self is one that loves the self unconditionally and from that core is able to love others and the world.

Therapy helps us recognize what needs attention and support within us to grow or change. It helps us determine what is the true self and what are adaptations or coping patterns that we no longer need. It's useful to borrow from the IFS repertoire when we talk about how creativity can help to re-establish the authentic self as the head of the inner family—overseeing the protectors, defenders, vulnerable parts, wounded inner child parts, and many others.

Any of these parts can become the artist that expresses through: dance, theatre, singing, music, writing, art or other creative outlets. We need our authentic self at the helm, choosing what's best for us in the moment-to-moment decision-making of our lives.

We must begin the fine detail of sorting out what's our authentic self and what are patterns or behaviours that we've taken on by default from others out of a need for connection or safety.

Repair and Return

How do we make sense of all this? How do we round up the parts, decide what to keep and cultivate, and what to release that is no longer useful to us?

How do we return to self after traumatic experiences have distorted our realities, disconnected us from ourselves, caused negative thoughts and beliefs about us and limited our belief in our basic goodness and potential for success and pleasure?

We need to prepare ourselves for the emergence of the split-off aspects of the self, or we won't know how to hold them when they arrive. We won't know how to integrate them. There are very good reasons why they were banished to a place of safe-keeping in the first place. It takes some convincing to reassure them that it's safe for them to re-emerge after years of hiding.

To see our authentic selves as separate from our wounded selves, we need to get emotional help for our wounded selves. We also need support for our authentic self so they can emerge and strengthen.

When we work with the exiled parts, energy and emotion are released from their "bound flow" states. Parts that were previously suspended in an inner limbo are finally able to reunite and be reintegrated with the self, moving it towards a sense of wholeness.

Attending to Creative Impulses – Healing and Rebuilding the Authentic Self

Creativity and emotional awareness are vital to living an integrated, fully satisfying life. When we have these elements in our lives we can then engage in relationships with other authentic beings. But the work starts with us. If we don't have deep, satisfying connection within ourselves then we search for what we are missing in others. This doesn't allow for the most satisfying relationships. We end up not living fully in the present and possibly blaming or exhausting our partners by trying to get from them something that we need from within ourselves.

Creativity allows us to explore the various options at play with no negative consequences resulting from of our choices. All options are on the table when we are working creatively. Whether we're moving, painting, acting, singing or writing there are no wrong answers or responses. One is encouraged to follow all impulses that arise leading to a strong, confident freedom and a sense of self that can then tackle life's challenges.

In dealing with trauma, Psychologist Bill O'Hanlon says it's like the two aspects of past and present are trying to get through a single door, and they're jammed in there together – they're stuck. They can't go forward or back. In therapy, he makes a double door and gives permission for both the stuck or frozen part and the moving, present part to be experienced simultaneously. Varying degrees of trauma cause different responses, and individuals will respond to similar situations from their unique character and disposition. Trauma in the environment may cause a tuning in to the outer world versus exploration of the inner life of the child affecting the natural development of the authentic self. Exploration of this inner life experience builds a personal, intimate sense of the artist within.

Our lives require a series of split second decision-making moments. Without connection to self – emotional, creative, spiritual – we lack the confidence to make strong intuitive choices.

Often we hear:

"I haven't got a creative bone in my body."
"I never could draw."
"I'm lousy at art."
"I have two left feet on the dance floor."
"I couldn't ... I haven't ... I'm bad at ... I'm lousy at ..."

Many of us have said similar things ourselves. We grew up believing we have nothing to share creatively with the world. Parents and teachers often reinforce these negative thoughts and beliefs about creativity by judging children and their creative work. Facial reactions, critical words or lack of a response can shut children down when they are in their most open and vulnerable states, when they've created something unique to them and are showing it proudly.

Teachers themselves are often not aware of their negative impact, due to their own limiting and negative experiences growing up in a similar relationship to their creativity. Teachers must follow rules and deliver a curriculum within a system that is evaluating them, in a culture that values intellect over creativity. Our imagination, intuition and instincts are often seen as secondary to the intellect. Teaching children to conform, follow rules and learn the contents of the curriculum is the main focus of education with art as a type of break activity from the important stuff. I think we have it very wrong. Just look to all innovation and new designs and advancements in any field and you will see artists at work. Why haven't we connected the dots ?

How Creativity Works in Healing from Negative Experiences

Limiting thoughts and beliefs are usually fear-based and false. We are all creative beings with infinite capacity. Whether one expresses it though cooking, love-making, house-building or through the arts—dance, theatre, music, writing—creativity is our most basic nature—to gather information from our world, ingest it, combine it in a unique way and present it back to the world.

Children are naturally creative, open, vulnerable, sensitive, curious and playful. In physically and emotionally safe environments they are free to explore who they are and how they relate to others and their world.

Educators need to get children out from behind their desks and encourage curiosity. They need to get children exploring, engaged, using their intuitive, creative impulses so often that it becomes second nature for them and they become strong, confident and secure in themselves.

There is a theatre improvisation exercise where two actors begin by one giving an opening line. The other has to pick up the line, support it, run with it and add something to it to create a story line. The minute one blocks the play, disagrees, or fails to receive what's been given, she is out of the improvisation and sits down and another actor jumps in. It shows very quickly how blocking and negative we can be without knowing it. If one actor says, "The sky is purple," another may add to the scene by saying, "Yes, it's very purple with a bank of fluffy mauve clouds rolling in from the south. I think it'll rain lilacs soon." Then it's over to the other actor for the next line, "We really should be rounding up vases and noses." Each person must fully accept the other's offering and add to it creatively to move the scene along.

This exercise unblocks the flow between actors, allowing them to receive spontaneously and creatively that which is given to them and build a relationship that is alive and dynamic and engaging with another actor. It makes for exciting theatre performed with generosity and confident strong teamwork—one of cooperation versus competition or comparison. The better my partner looks, the more support I receive and the more we have to play with. Switching from comparison and competition to cooperation is a key to fostering creative confidence in children, youth and adults of all ages.

With a background of having taught movement and physical theatre, plus having done my own therapy for over 25 years, I began training as a psychotherapist. I had seen how easily movement and creativity can trigger deep, unresolved emotions. A small amount of movement can open up *Pandora's Box* of unresolved material inside of us. It's best to be aware of that 'potency' and get emotional support or the social support of a group, if possible. It's not weak to ask for help – it takes courage. It will allow you to go deeper, heal further and faster.

I know of many success stories where creativity and body work reached in and healed parts of the self where talking alone couldn't reach. Feelings live in the body, and the body lives in the present. Life is lived in the present; the rest is memory or illusion. Hearing the words 'present moment' and experiencing it are two very different things. Our mind can have an idea of what that means, but without help to get there and feel it for yourself, you will only have an intellectual concept of what that means. Emilie Conrad, from Continuum, used to differentiate it by saying, "It's only the map, not the territory," meaning were offering you a structure you make it a transformative experience.

We have to know when to slow down, pause or reach out for help from someone we trust. Then we can welcome all our parts – including the scared ones. We can respect their fear and build trusting relationships that integrate and repair the self.

We all know we 'should' have self-love, another concept that is bantered about—but self-love is out of reach for many of us, no matter how much we read, listen to lectures, or enroll in online seminars. We need presence in action in a safe space that can hold us when we can't do it for ourselves. We need someone who loves and respects that part of us that we reject until we can build healthier relationships with it, lift off the blankets of shame and judgment and quiet ourselves. Only then can we get down to the vulnerable level of the self, when we feel surrounded by emotional safety and compassion, acceptance and warmth. Then we can build a tolerance for the content held in these banished parts of the self that we hold within our body tensions, emotions and energy.

Man hours of *Authentic Movement* over many years has given me an awareness of what being in the present moment actually is. If one has experienced trauma, that present moment isn't always accessible or pleasant. It can be painful, frightening and difficult, but when we show up to the moment with self-compassion and curiosity, our level of tolerance increases. We can then become the explorers of our own inner landscape.

In clown we describe a place "between the panic and the possibilities" where the possibilities are infinite. Marion Woodman describes us as 'infinite beings in finite bodies." If you're reading this, maybe it's time for you to connect through head, heart and gut and go deeper, explore more. Remember to find a buddy and don't swim alone. Your Self is waiting. She's been ever so patient.

The following exercises present a pathway to a deeper connection with the self through writing, movement and art. Take them at your own pace, paying attention to what appeals to you. There is no wrong choice or way in. Always bear in mind your safety and that of others.

Chapter 5 Exploring Trauma

Writing

Body Paper

To write your body paper, find a comfortable place where you can write, uninterrupted for at least one hour, but no longer than three.

Write the history of your body, its agonies and ecstasies. If you get stuck along the way you can gain access through a scar. A scar can be interpreted to mean many things. It could be physical (a tonsillectomy) or emotional (a fearful incident) an intellectual thought or belief (I'm not worth listening to) or spiritual (God punishes tardy children) There is crossover with each of the categories so don't be overly concerned with getting it 'right' or what category it falls into. Whatever lands and feels right for you.

Begin anywhere. Go anywhere. Trust your intuition. Work from what is showing up now. Be curious. What's tugging on the shirttails of your intuitive self? Inquire with an open mind and body. Lean into your impulses and welcome whatever shows up however foreign it might feel. Find out what fuels them, keeps them alive.

Probe further, explore more. The possibilities are infi-nite.

Variation - Voice Paper

Same as the Body Paper, only now it's your voice. Write the history of your voice, it's agony and ecstasy.

If you can't decide where to go or if you get bogged down or overwhelmed, list your options on a sheet of paper, close your eyes and feel for the one to do next. Run your fingers down the list and stop when you feel it in your body. Remember, it's the same river of cre-ativity that you're jumping into whether you enter on one side or the other, upstream or down.

Let the rest of the items on the list know that you will get back to them, and ask them to be patient. Thank them for showing up. This acknowledgement will go a long way towards keeping the flow open for future writes. Make sure that you do, eventually, get back to them.

The acknowledgment and gratitude will help these parts that have been waiting for you to come for them for a very long time. Remember there are no mistakes or wrong answers.

I learned the above exercise from Linda Putnam, my physical theatre teacher. It took me on a profound creative, emotional, healing journey. I've introduced this exercise to students and clients over the years with equally profound results.

One student wrote a body paper during a class that I was teaching at a summer theatre intensive at Queens University in Kingston. She wrote about her traumatic history of family abuse and the resulting addictions that were her way of coping. Her body paper was full of pain and suffering, but it also had moments of humour in it. I couldn't stop chuckling as I read it, even while wiping away tears. Her humour held the tragic reality of her life. In a feedback session with her, I shared my reactions to the piece, both the trauma and the fun.

She knew her suffering and pain so deeply but hadn't seen the humour in her writing before. Creative doors swung open for her. She found a new writing voice, body energy and creative momentum. She continued to work on her piece, developing it into a one-woman show. It was energetic, funny and packed a punch.

Through this process, she transformed her trauma through her creative writing, healing herself along the way. This process broke the negative hold her trauma had on her mentally, emotionally and physically. She could now stop repeating past traumatic patterns and move the trapped emotions out of her system. She was in charge, delivering her truth in a way that her audiences could both laugh and cry with her, see aspects of themselves in her performance and gain hope for their own healing. Having witnesses to see her pain and, as importantly, the humour in her writing allowed her to spin her straw into gold.

What straw needs spinning into gold in your life?

Visual Art

Sculpture - Blindfolded Sculpting

A visual art exercise I love to teach is blindfolded sculpting. You will need a piece of clay. I like to use a grapefruit-sized piece of clay but any size could work.

Sit in a comfortable position and put on your blindfold. Breathe, feel the ground beneath your feet, and hold the clay in your hands. Smell it, feel its texture, warm it up and begin to knead it until it's soft and pliable. Begin to sculpt your body. Don't worry about accurate proportions or how good it will be or how it compares with others. Let go of that mental chatter if you can and drop in underneath it.

You may choose to sculpt your whole body or an abstract impression of your body—how it feels and moves—anything that calls to you. Take your time.

Keep dropping in beneath the critics and the expectations, and have fun. Connect with the clay as an extension of the self as much as you can. There is no best result. The one that appears is the best one.

Have the clay on a piece of white bond paper or craft paper. When you feel complete take your blindfold off and sit with your first impressions. Try not to judge it. Free associate with the piece – creatively what comes to mind - song lyrics, poetry, impressions, images, textures. Write them down on the paper, using a pencil or crayon. Continue to write your creative associations until you feel complete. Take the words you've written and connect them together making an intuitive poem or story. If you are doing this in a group with others, each participant can sit with each clay piece and free associate so that when you return to your piece of clay you have the creative associations of others as well as your own.

Share your findings together in a group, and reflect on the whole process for yourself and with others.

Trauma shatters our sense of inner wholeness, fracturing us into parts. Creativity can pick up our split off parts and reunite them with our core self. As you build a deeper and fuller connection with the self, remember to be grateful to the parts of you that show up and explore so bravely. And to those parts that turn away and hide tell them that's OK too. They may not be ready. Tell them you'll wait and that you understand. Offer compassion, compassion, and then more compassion.

Chapter 6

Creativity and Anger

Taming the Dragon -
Working Creatively with Anger

We all have anger in our lives. It is a vital emotion related to getting our important needs met, such as the need for safety and belonging. Anger can be a gold mine of information for the individual. It is our fire, our passion and our protector and defender.

I often see anger as a dragon at the mouth of the cave protecting its young inside. Its young are our needs. We need to feel safe and seen, feel we belong, are valued, that we connect deeply within and with others. We need to feel that we are in control of our lives with the power to decide what's best for us short and long term. So how can we tame the dragon? The dragon calms down when our needs are met and we feel safe.

Many people disown their own needs as well as the needs of others. These people often dislike 'needy' people. But not recognizing and honouring their legitimate individual needs isolates those needs still further. This situation may cause a host of problematic secondary emotions such as shame, blame, guilt or negative judgment.

We try so hard to deny or push anger away or "not have anger," eliminating access to much of our vibrant, fiery, passionate energy. And it takes a lot of energy to deny anger. If we expend our energy repressing and denying our anger to feel likeable, strong, protected and safe, then there's less energy left for living a vital life.

But we were taught from childhood to suppress our anger: anger wasn't socially acceptable. We understood that we weren't good people if we felt anger, and we were worse people if we expressed it. You can see how it became suppressed. Anger was not allowed.

A parent's anger that feels out of control to a child leaves that child in fear for their very survival and terrified. Parents wield anger as a threat to control children's behaviours.

In my high school classroom, we had the dreaded yardstick that would strike our desk with a resounding *crack* beside our ears as a warning. In public school, the principal's strap was another example. This kind of violence leaves scars, both physical and emotional. Luckily times have changed, and it isn't happening as often anymore. Parents have access to more knowledge of the harm it can do. We still have a distance to go before we eliminate and replace these behaviours with better ones.

Some people become stuck in anger, using it as their first response to everything even intimacy and pleasure. These people are robbed of a life that has emotional variety in it. Picture a piano player limited to playing one key – that's the metaphor for someone who responds to every situation with the same emotion.

Other individuals are unable to express any anger, even when it would be in their best interests to do so. Fear is often closely attached to anger for these individuals. As children, they may have experienced expressing anger as dangerous, since expressing it then caused the threat of punishment or abandonment by a parent or guardian. When anger isn't an option, it goes underground where it gets expressed subversively.

In contrast, pure anger cuts through defences and leaves the sender bare and vulnerable. It comes from a place of love and desire to reach the other, who is an important person in the sender's life. Anger can launch us into action, becoming a force for change in the world.

Much of the expression of our anger as adults is a toxic, impure anger where we project our hurt and abandonment onto others, making them responsible for our pain and loneliness from the past. We had no power as a child to get our needs met so now we exert pseudo power in adult relationships to try to get from our partners what we didn't get earlier, by protesting, demanding, coercing and manipulating, 'I didn't get something as a child so I expect you to give it to me now, or you'll be sorry.'

We are notorious for projecting our needs onto others, expecting them to take care of those needs for us; then we blame them when they fail and we aren't happy.

Often couples run into conflict when they unwittingly try to get their childhood needs met by their partners in their adult relationships. Anger between partners is almost always an attempt to connect and communicate something to the important person in their lives. It's about being seen and heard, understood and cared for. Usually couples do care and want to support each other, they just don't know how. With help it all becomes clear for them. Anger is usually the sand that grates the oyster, creating a pearl.

Moving back and forth between our internal messages 'Get away, get away, get away, come here, come here, come here,' is an interesting dance to explore. 'I need you and I need my space,' 'Leave me alone, but don't leave me,' are often positions that appear to be contradictory, but both are true. As a couple, coordinating the right amount of time spent together and apart is the challenge.

Finding balance within the self for alone time and social time can also be a challenge. Some people spend too much time alone and others over-fill their time to avoid feelings. The balance of this is unique to each individual and their particular needs at the moment. What brings one person pleasure brings another sorrow. It's worth getting in touch with how to monitor the inner balance one needs for alone time and connection with others. These imbalances often lead to anger or other expressions of discontent.

It often takes the help of a couple's therapist to identify these unrecognized and unmet needs as the underlying triggers for anger or other expressions of discontent.

Needs vary from individual to individual and couple to couple. Our needs as individuals and partners also change over time. We take our cars to the mechanic for check-ups, water our gardens regularly in the summer, and continuously refresh and reboot our computers, but we tend to be less aware of what is needed to keep our emotional lives fresh and healthy. Regular emotional check-ins are also required, as our needs are fluid and changing.

So how can we do an emotional check-in?

First, each one of us must determine what our specific needs are and which ones we might be disconnected from and which are lacking in our lives. Many of us are unable to recognize what's lacking. Longing and anger are indicators of this internal discontent. If instead of getting swept away by those emotions, we can just see them as flags that some need is not being met, then we can follow the clues to get in touch with what is wanting. Often we need help to discover what needs we have that we might not be aware of.

If we have never had love and acceptance or security, we may not be fully aware of the way that plays out in our lives. Our adaptation may be one of "I don't need anyone, I'm happy alone and self-sufficient. I'm fearless." When we look further, there is a longing and need for connection, safety and validation. Professional counselling can help one discover those needs in a safe container where acceptance and support for all needs are modelled by the therapist. I'm not saying that people cannot be entirely happy and alone, for they most certainly can.

Anger vs. Rage – The Difference

John Lee, in *Facing the Fire and The Anger Solution*, has contributed extensively to our understanding of anger. He differentiates between anger and rage.

"Anger lives in the present, and so takes minutes to be felt and expressed. Rage sticks around because it is grounded in the past. Anger is about me and rage is about you. If I'm expressing Anger, I'm telling you about me. Anger is revealing. If I'm raging, I'm telling the other person about them, and thus I am concealing what I am really feeling and going through."

Anger is a healthy emotion like sorrow or happiness. Rage is considered unhealthy and a mix of fear, desperation, anger and panic. Anger is a response when one is feeling offended or wronged, threatened or slighted. An angry person has the power to control their emotions. In contrast, an enraged person has no control and can become destructive. Anger doesn't end in bloodshed; rage might.

Anger's associates are shame, guilt, blame and judgment. We might get angry at our partner, lash out, then feel ashamed and judge ourselves for being so unloving or worse, label ourselves as an unloving person unworthy of love. We explored these secondary emotions in Chapter 3 - Blocks to Creativity. Right now we'll stay with the exploration of anger and its relationship to needs.

Working Creatively with Anger

When I worked with the violence curriculum in theatre, I required actors develop a strong skill base to support them through the dramatization of fights and attacks without physical or mental harm to themselves and others. There was no room for 'blind rage' on stage as it threatened the safety of the individual and cast. It also broke the illusion of theatre for the audience.

Blind rage is a real concern when training for theatre or improvisation. I have seen rage triggered in theatre training where an actor becomes blind in the moment because his or her history is activated. They need help to get through the scene clearly so that safety is maintained. I once had to ask an actor to leave a course I was teaching when his rage was so present, yet so unconscious, that he posed a threat to the safety of others. Of course my meeting with him was done privately and lovingly with great respect. That inner condition wasn't generated spontaneously from his personality; he had been through trauma in his past where he had picked up rage as a defence mechanism. But in that particular situation he needed a trained professional to help him with that rage.

When we are prone to rage, we have learned to protect ourselves by using it. We need to learn how to go into vulnerable feelings such as fear and sorrow, and the needs that are beneath the anger in an emotionally safe container. We need to learn how to contain the intense feelings of needing to attack others, the world or ourselves. I have helped clients contain their rage and be with it with compassion. Tears of sadness and isolation usually come with a feeling of vulnerability and needs that were never met and now have to be attended to. Slowing down, taking long, deep breaths, pausing the argument and feeling what's underneath the rage is a place to start. This isn't an easy thing to do when we're in the middle of rage. But vulnerable feelings beneath the rage is where we eventually need to go – to tears and to connection. When you feel heard and safe, the rage isn't needed as a protector or defender.

Anger is a gold mine. The benefits of working creatively with anger are many. If you use these techniques and exercises to get consciously in touch with anger it's possible to work through it to a life that feels much better. Then anger is just another vein of gold to explore.

Chapter 6 Exercises For Anger

Exploring Body Shapes - Twisted, Gnarled

A good place to start our warm-up for anger exploration is with tension and release. Tense the muscles, hold for a count of 4 or 5 and then release them. This is best done lying down, but not imperative.

1. Travel through the body – front side, back side, right side, left side, upper, lower, inner, outer, face, scalp, diagonal right arm/left leg, left arm/right leg, fingers, toes ankles, wrists, etc. until the whole body feels tensed, held and released. Then add a bit of easy shaking of the muscles in those various body parts to loosen any remaining tension. Squeeze the breath and release it as well; if there is sound on the release all the better. In a group setting I might have people partner up and give each other an easy body massage, kneading, patting, rolling out each others' arms, legs or back to bring one fully into the body, ready to explore the physicality of anger and need.

Now we are ready to explore the body shape of twisted/gnarled. Imagine your body as a gnarly tree branch. Twist your fingers, toes, arms, legs, torso, neck, face, and lips—whatever you can find to twist and bend with. The nature of a twist in the body is that one part goes in one direction while another goes in an opposing direction all at once. Let yourself twist into a new shape and release out of it as you did in the tension and release warm-up. Don't stay too long in twisted shapes. Let them breathe, moving in and out of them as your body desires. Add sound on the exhale if it feel right to you.

What sounds do these twisted shapes want to make from the body? If these shapes could travel through the space how would that look? If they meet and interact with other twisted shapes how would that look? If they feel defensive and threatened by the other twisted shapes so they need to hide or defend themselves how would that look?

*Take a rest and draw, paint or write the experience,
then share your findings with the group.*

Effort Actions in Movement

Two of Rudolf Laban's "effort actions" that are effective in exploring anger are slash and punch. Both are heavy in their weight, and fast in terms of timing; the punch is direct and specific in space while the slash is indirect and less distinct. For a more complete description of the *eight effort actions* by Rudolf Laban, see entry in the Endnotes.

> *2. Explore the actions of slashing, or punching using not just your fist or hand but other body parts as well such as an elbow or a knee or a foot or hip. Add a forceful sound, like a karate kiai, its battle cry. Be a deadly threat and indestructible. Become the legendary Bruce Lee.*

It is important that you don't physically hurt yourself while doing this. For example if an actor who is following impulse in the violence curriculum punches a wall, the initial impulse of aggression is instantly transformed into pain and the initial impulse of aggression is lost. If one *"slips the screen"* as Linda Putnam called it in physical theatre or pulls the punch just short of hitting the wall then the impulse returns to the actor and he or she gains momentum.

> *3. The action can then be repeated with more energy and possibly adding sound to it. Each of these actions; punching, stomping or slashing can travel through space and have sound added. Each can have a character develop out of the exploration. These characters can interrelate, improvising in movement, adding gibberish—a nonsensical language based on sound and gesture—or one word dialogue or short phrases or*

more. For more on Gibberish see "Catherine Marrion on Gibberish" in the Endnotes.

This exercise be recorded by others on a recording device and be used for writing purposes and scene development later on. Collages might be created capturing costume ideas or story lines for further exploration.

I've used texts for exploring anger: these lines are from Shakespeare's King Lear.

Blow, winds and crack you cheeks! rage! blow!...spit fire!

It's a great passage to connect with one's power and force.

Another text I've used comes from Linda Putnam. I'm not sure of her source. It's a simple ditty that accesses anger and frustration followed by love and affection. It's fun to repeat over and over and to play around with. I used this as a closing each day on my creativity and fear course entitled "Where Angels Fear to Tread". Participants were then able to leave the workshop, after an intense day, on a balanced note.

It goes like this;

I hate that egg, gonna kick out the chicken, ain't never gonna eat another egg in my life.

I love that egg, gonna feed up the chickens, I'm gonna live another day of my life.

Another improvisation I have used I simply call Sushi. It is done in twos using gibberish where both people play sumo wrestlers with a plate of sushi between them.

Theatre - How Aggression Relates

> *1. There is only one piece of sushi left on the plate and each wrestler is saying to the other—in gibberish of course so it's nonsensical— "You have it," gesturing to the last piece of sushi on the plate. The other insists, "No, you have it." It goes back and forth with energy building into a conflict. One isn't allowed to resolve the improv by eating or chopping the sushi in half. It's so much fun to play through frustration as a sumo wrestler insisting on being the more generous one.*

Depending on the participants needs, histories and tolerance for aggression, the following exercises are taken from theatre. They may need to be adapted or may not be appropriate for certain situations.

> *2. Another exercise I've used for aggression work with actors begins with two people facing each other, each with a hand drum and a beater held out in front of the body. The goal of the game is to hit the other person's drum. In between these attempts, each person beats their own drum moving around the space trying to trick or fool their opponent into letting down their guard in order to score the winning point. The energy builds, as does the aggression. Note; this exercise needs to be controlled so that no one gets hurt.*

> *3. Two actors can explore anger using the statement, "I hate you" back and forth trying to outdo each other in passion and energy brought to the moment's expression. Who is more convincing? It becomes clear as the game goes on that one wins. Then it is switched to one*

117

speaking, "I hate you" while the other says, "I love you" in response. Then the roles are reversed. Or one says, "I hate you" and the other says "I don't believe you" until they feel fully convinced of their partners words at which time they say, "I believe you" and then it gets reversed.

One has to dig for the emotion and energy of anger in order to deliver a believable statement of anger or hatred or, in this case, extreme anger, but not rage. Remember rage is something else, and for safety reasons, the improv stops if rage shows up.

Language - Anger/Need Inquiry

Working with a partner is best but you can do this individually as well. Repeat the question to your partner "How does your anger express itself?" Or if you're doing the exercise alone, "How does my anger express itself?" Record the answer in a notebook and say "thank-you" then repeat the question again. If in pairs, the partner asking the question may record the other's answers. Continue for 5-10 minutes depending upon the energy generated by the exercise. Then take a break and reverse the roles. Once both people have their answers, reflect on these statements and use one that resonates with you as a prompt for a 30 minute write.

Other repeating questions might be;

"What do you need?"
"When I'm angry I _____"
"When I'm needy I _____"
"When others are angry (or needy) I _____"

Remember to record the other's responses and say thank you after each response. Go slowly so as not to rush your partner. Make sure they are finished before saying thank you and speaking again. Have them nod to indicate when they are finished speaking; this helps you to know when to speak.

Continue this inquiry for an agreed upon period of time, 5-7 minutes is a good length of time to begin with. Take this into an extended write of 30 minutes or more on what stands out for you from this inquiry. Share your findings and physically move the response through the body or onto a sheet of paper using colours and textures or collage it using images from magazines. Make sure to conclude the exploration in a grounded way where you feel fully present and back to the here and now, seeing, hearing, smelling and feeling the physical surroundings before returning to daily tasks such as driving.

We had a saying in theatre, *'only go in as far as you know how to get back.'* This is especially important to remember when delving into and exploring anger. It needs a secure container holding its exploration. Baby steps are best with an adult part of you in charge, driving the bus. Working with a buddy or having a professional available if you need it is a good self-care plan. Stop and reach out if you begin to feel ungrounded, overwhelmed or lost.

Chapter 7

Creativity and Fear

Facing Fear, Finding Creative Treasure

F ear is the most vulnerable of the raw emotions. It plays an important role in keeping us safe from harm.

There are a number of different kinds of fear. There is fear in response to facing a real-life, present-time danger. If we are walking down the street at night and we hear footsteps coming up behind us we could register potential danger in our bodies and step into a store and call for a ride. Our bodies return to a non-fearful, resting state once we've resolved the threatening situation.

Most of the time the fear we experience isn't in response to a real life threat. The vast majority of fear experienced by people is fear that is imagined. It's accompanied by thoughts of past or future potentially threatening situations which are not happening in the present moment.

This worst-case scenario thinking that attempts to handle possible threats can become debilitating for people. Their world may become smaller and smaller. Their bodies become stuck in anxious or terrified states where they are constantly reacting to frightening situations that don't actually exist,at least, not at the present moment. Or they vigilantly avoid any potentially triggering situations and therefore aren't able to live in the present moment comfortably.

The *reptilian brain* or *instinctual brain*, is the first area of the brain to develop in the womb. The primary drive of the reptilian brain is survival so it is highly attuned to anything that may be perceived as a threat.

Sensations felt in the body in response to threat, whether the threat is current or remembered, are messages from the instinctual brain. Our *neocortex,* or thinking brain, is quick to label our sensations and emotions in an attempt to explain away or control any discomfort or sense of threat. This speedy thinking response can rob us of a full experience whether it is in art making or in our social or personal lives.

Intense body sensations can trigger a shutdown. But they can also be messengers of opportunity and excitement concerning what's about to happen. Two actors who are preparing to go on stage may experience the same felt sensations in their bodies, such as butterflies in the belly, sweaty palms or a tight jaw. One actor begins to worry, thinking these bodily sensations herald that she's in trouble, she's losing control. She becomes full of fear saying, "I'm going to blow it, forget my lines, and flop big time." The other actor, experiencing similar sensations, says, "Oh goody! I feel pumped. I'm going to have a great show." The same sensations with very different associations, interpretations and relationships create dramatically different results.

Difference Between Anxiety and Fear

Sometimes our response to fear is not anxiety but a "numbing out". I watched the horror film "The Mummy," with a friend years ago and had nightmares afterwards. The next day when I told him about having nightmares his response was, "Oh, are you ever lucky!" as if nightmares were a good thing that extended the bounty of the horror film. He loved horror. It left him feeling more alive when he connected with fear in his body through horror films. I concluded his own fear from the past was inaccessible to him, and horror films were a way to try to find a lost part of himself.

Shutting down and disconnecting is one way many people cope when they've had a traumatic past. Anxiety is another coping mechanism – it's an attempt to manage present dangers or prepare for future ones. Both of these coping strategies have a cost to them.

The difference between anxiety and fear is that anxiety is a state, whereas fear is pure emotion. Within the state of anxiety, there are thoughts, beliefs, feelings and sensations that are whirling around with tornado-like energy that gathers momentum as it goes. It's like a campfire that one keeps throwing logs onto until it becomes a blazing inferno that's out of control and the area has to be evacuated. The scary "what if" thoughts contribute to the condition we end up in, which is overwhelmed and suffering.

Anxiety is a coping strategy — albeit not the most effective one. It attempts to prepare us for what is to come that may be even scarier than what we're feeling right now. Ninety-nine per cent of the time we're wrong; we've run ourselves through a rigorous gauntlet of heightened thought, feeling and sensation for nothing.

These deep patterns of survival run on autopilot within the psyche but don't actually help us prepare for difficult situations. They exhaust and deplete our reserves, removing us from the present moment. Just the other day I referred to the container of tulips in my office and said we can enjoy the beauty of those tulips as they are now knowing they will die in a week and be gone or we can be sad or disappointed or frightened or angry every day knowing that they will die and be robbed of the enjoyment of their beauty in the present. These emotions can hijack our lives, our happiness and our peace of mind.

There are a wide variety of techniques that can help us manage anxiety. Once anxiety is under control then we can go deeper into the underlying fear that is driving the anxiety on the surface above it. Once we locate and embrace that deeper fear it can be expressed through creativity and the emotional, energetic pressure can be released so it no longer drives our actions.

Creative activities geared to explore those coping patterns and to feel into the fear, knowing one is in control and choosing to do so, rewires the nervous system and de-activates certain neural pathways that wire and fire together when stimulated. We couple these firings with another experience, one of safety, humour, praise, comfort, support or courage. The fear then loses its power to scare us and drive our actions negatively.

How to Deal with Fear –
Talk Therapy & Creative Solutions

Talk therapy helps us to understand with our intellects some very important information concerning our patterns of adaptation and responses to past and present events and the people involved. It can help the heart open and the body feel more present and alive. Bioenergetics and somatic therapies work with the physical and energetic bodies, our emotions and sensations.

Creativity can take our patterns of adaptation and sculpt them into something different, something brand new and valuable. It can spin straw into gold, pain into laughter, anger into passion, sorrow into a thing of beauty. I look at some of my art and see my pain transformed into something quite new that has power, beauty and spirit shining through. That is transformative.

The way talk therapy, body-centred psychotherapy and creativity work with fear are quite different. I value talk therapy for building strategies in the beginning of therapy that the client can take away and use in moments when they need them.

In talk therapy, people verbally recall situations in which they felt frightened and how they coped with them at the time. We may discuss coping strategies and develop resources for managing similar situations more effectively in the future. It is valuable to equip clients with a set of coping strategies they can use in their day to day lives to help manage fear, anxiety, panic or phobias. These are useful to have until the root cause of the fear is addressed and repaired.

I have different strategies that I offer clients depending on which level their fear is occupying, be it intellectual (fearful thoughts) or physical/energetic (butterflies in the belly). We determine what strategies they already have in place for coping with fear and reinforce these first. It is often reassuring for the client to hear an external acknowledgment of the coping skills they already possess — everyone has some in place. Once these are named, appreciated and validated we can add to the list or refine what they're using.

For example, if fear is showing up as fearful thoughts and going into the body only exasperates it, then the 5-4-3-2-1 tool is a simple, effective method to regain one's grounding into the present moment without stirring further emotion and energy in an already anxious body. This exercise is described in detail at the end of this chapter.

———————

When anxiety shows up as scary thoughts clients are often imagining a worst-case scenario that hasn't happened yet. I get them to challenge those "What if ..." negative outcome thoughts with an "On the other hand what if ..." positive outcome.

"What if I lose my job?"

"On the other hand what if I don't?"

Then, using Byron Katie's method from *The Work*, I ask them, "How do you feel when you think the first thought? And how do you feel when you think the second thought? If you could choose one or the other, since they are both imagined, which would it be?"

The client understands that the first thought is scaring them: they learn to stay in the present and not go into the future. They learn to choose thoughts that help them feel safe, rather than frightened. They also recognize that if they had a friend or a child they would never give the same messages to their loved ones that they give to themselves. Building awareness stops rampant thoughts that only serve to frighten us and are not the reality of the moment. Often just asking "Is that true?" will yield an answer that is "No" and defuse scary thoughts.

I use metaphor and visual images in my practice to stimulate the imagination or right brain, offering creative responses and additional resources to the client.

Scary thoughts are like a horse drawn wagon with a driver who has dropped the reigns and a horse that has taken off in a full gallop; or scary thoughts are like someone who has hijacked the bus you're on and is taking off with it. Even worse, the hijacker is often a terrified, inner two year old or five year old or a pre-license disturbed teen. You don't want any of these driving the vehicle that's carrying you.

The same holds true when the physical body is addressed. There are three areas of brain functioning - the *neocortex* or thinking brain, the *limbic* or emotional brain, and the *reptilian* or instinctual brain.

In bottom-up versions of therapy, the intellect is not leading the session as it often does in top down therapy. It is riding in the back seat listening and observing the emotional/instinctual patterns of behaviour while trying to make sense of them. The intellect would like to think it's always in control and the smartest of all systems but the instincts are usually what is driving the bus whether we like it or not. The sooner we realize that the better off we are. The thinking brain is best used to talk other terrified parts of us off the ledge, or to grab the reigns of our runaway horse or step into the driver's seat of our bus and slow things down. If we can recognize when we are in *fright, flight or freeze* mode, our conscious self can regulate this runaway part by saying something calming or performing actions that comfort, soothe and settle us.

We can also build resources on the physical/energetic level for clients who feel fear. If fear is presenting on a physical level — butterflies, anxiety, panic, chills, shaking, aches, tension in the body — we address it at the level of the body rather than with thought. I have clients slow things down by breathing to the count of five, saying, "I'm breathing in, two, three, four, five. I'm breathing out, two, three, four, five."

I also help clients get grounded by bringing their attention to the present moment. Feeling the floor, its texture beneath their feet, describing the sensation of the carpet or their foot in their shoe can be grounding.

In therapy we build up a tolerance for sensation while re-visiting past frightening events and feelings that are stored in the body, bringing attention to these parts that are stuck in the past holding traumatic experiences. By bringing a new supportive resource to these parts, it changes the locked-in-place pattern and releases the charge, allowing an integration of the energy and emotion that is tied to the past event. The goal is to bring all parts out of suspended separateness into an experience of wholeness and integration.

I draw from my *Authentic Movement* and *Continuum* training for ways to be present with sensation in the body bringing curiosity and inquiry to the moment without the need to label or move to narrative. For example I can meet butterflies in the solar plexus and be with them, curious about them, breathing and moving with them, without needing to know what they mean or linking them to any upcoming event with my thoughts.

What if we could just sit with the butterflies and bring our attention, curiosity and inquiry that stays to the sensations, only thinking, "That's interesting, tell me more." Then we can stay with the message from the body, possibly offering to comfort, sooth and settle it if the intensity becomes too great just as we would with a friend, or as parent would do with a child.

Ask, *"What would I say or do if my best friend or child was in this state and came to me for help?"* The answer is often crystal clear without a doubt.

Most of my clients know how to be with others in this situation but are unable to offer it to themselves in a moment of panic. Just the acknowledgment of that begins to build an inner resource that can be useful in times of need.

We need to build inner relationships that are as strong and confident in their actions as our outer ones. Self-love begins with being kind and supportive to ourselves in times when we're scared.

I refer to two energy medicine exercises from Donna Eden to help with this, Expelling the Venom and The Zip Up. The first clears out the negative, toxic energy from the body and the second builds the container of the body, insulating it from exterior, intrusive energy. These can be found on YouTube.

Artist's Blocks Due to Fear

Most fear is historic in nature in that it's stored in the body from past experiences. Over time certain events trigger it and it surfaces in an attempt to be resolved and integrated into the self, versus being held apart from the self—in exile.

When triggered, the mind takes off like a wildfire, hijacking the present moment in an attempt at keeping the person safe and out of harm's way. Unfortunately it has the opposite effect, keeping the person away from being in the present, centred and grounded.

We have only the present moment, it is the home of our greatest power. Everything else is just mental/emotional static clouding our experience, robbing us of the beauty and passion that's available to us every moment.

My own experience and understanding of presence has come through movement, theatre, voice and art. Creativity anchors us in the present, allowing us to repurpose past events funnelling them through a new lens or interpretation where new meaning is given to old memories. New mental/emotional links or *neural pathways* are created. Past trauma can become a comedian's present-day performance or a bold and vibrant abstract painting or a powerful scene in the play that an actor is writing.

Translation through creativity gives power and control back to the individual out of the hands of the event or the perpetrator of the injury. I can't imagine life without creativity yet many people do not give themselves outlets for creative expression believing they aren't creative. Many people believe creativity isn't for them. That they just can't draw, dance, write, sing or whatever.

Not all art is meant to take you on a personal growth or healing journey and that's just fine. For the purposes of this book, we address the art that has this potential. Everyone is in some form of relationship with creativity, whether it's as a baker, gardener, builder, lover, artist, mover or actor. Anyone who think they aren't creative has been led to that belief through past experience. They're blocked. Dig a little deeper and you find an injury in need of repair and creative potential waiting to be discovered.

An overactive inner protector in a stuck fear/safety mode may paralyze us. It's over protection blocks us from our creative explorations. It's like a parent who locks a teenager in her room after one bad encounter with an unbounded boy. Instead of teaching her how to protect herself, how to exercise healthy boundaries and how to be out in the world with better protection, the fear locks her up and throws away the key.

We need the skills to know how to protect ourselves so that we are free to explore all that life offers, within a container of safety. Then fear becomes just a signal telling us that we are getting close to something exciting. Body sensations can trigger a shutdown or can indicate excitement and opportunity.

When we feel fear in the body we know it's a sign to slow down and pay attention. We need to remind ourselves that "We've got this, we're safe." Then we're free to explore the possibilities presenting themselves and discover the riches in what's showing up.

As an adult I was given a *Rorschach* test and told I scored higher in a category of early childhood fear than the seasoned therapist had ever seen. What that looked like was my description of scary faces that I saw in the inkblots that went on for so long that the clinician had to end each unit and move on or I would have stayed indefinitely on the first page of the test. I believe this explains my creative capacity to go deep and get lost in art, as well as my need to distract and avoid art due to the fear that I meet when I go there.

Exploring one's self and one's art can be a vulnerable thing to do. Theatre improvisation and clown are two of the places where I have experienced my fear most directly and worked to befriend it. "The further you choose to delve in and explore your fears the braver and more fearless you become."

As artists we need to push boundaries, discovering the zone that challenges us, but doesn't overwhelm us. As an audience member you can see the performers or artists who give themselves permission to play creatively, beyond their comfort zone. They push the boundaries. Great teachers encourage this in their students.

Ben Woolfitt, a visual artist and friend, did a similar thing for me with my paintings by suggesting, "This painting looks like it needs to be much bigger — maybe 6 feet." I hadn't ever imagined painting that large at that time. It blew open an inner door to a whole new body of art for me.

I recall a specific drawing by a client. It was a huge mallet hovering over a tiny daisy, ready to obliterate it in any second. She is now an artist attending Toronto School of Art creating powerful art, exhibiting in shows and proud of her work. She could never have tolerated the exposure in the past; it would have felt too unsafe to do so. She would not have been able to live her life as the artist and creator without therapy, the mallet and the daisy showed her the way.

Performers who play out on a creative edge where they no longer fear failure or shame or embarrassment are performers who have done a lot of improvisation or clown work, fallen on their faces so often that it no longer frightens them.

As I am making a piece of art, I'm not concentrating on the product or outcome. I'm moving physically and making decisions intuitively from the body, tapping into energy and emotional flow. I connect with the emotion and sensations, possibly grief or terror or laughter. I welcome it all.

This kind of art-making is intense, which explains the avoidance and blocking patterns we get into around doing it regularly. It has the potential to surprise, hijack and drag us into overwhelming emotions. I've talked about this in my chapter on Creativity and Trauma. I've felt emotionally

132

overwhelmed in my own creative life when feelings and sensations had become so intense I felt I could burst into flames, or lose control, ending up as a pile of cold ash. Other feelings are ones where I felt that I might explode from the sheer force of concentration into a thousand tiny particles flying through the universe. I have encountered similar descriptions of the creative process from clients in my therapy practice. These seem to be universal descriptions of the fear that may be experienced in the creative process.

We can also feel more alive through creativity in ways that no other activity comes close to offering us.

Emilie Conrad of *Continuum* movement used to say, "*Continuum* is lessons in making love with yourself." Creativity offers us an opportunity to know, integrate and transform all parts of ourselves – the good, the bad, and the ugly.

Vulnerability leads to depth connection, intimacy and love but it needs a safe container and others whom one can trust. Creativity can offer the environment in which we are free to explore our vulnerability and our feelings and expand and grow.

The following exercises are designed to gently build a tolerance for sensations in the body related to fears you may have. Go slowly maintaining awareness of the fact that you are in charge of the moment. How far, how long, how deep you go is up to you. Be kind and non-judgemental of yourself if you need to, slow down or stop. This will build your capacity to go deeper. Trust and safety are vital to this process.

Chapter 7 Exploring Fear

5-4-3-2-1 Grounding Through the Senses

One looks around the room or surroundings and identifies one thing you see, saying it aloud if you can, to yourself or silently if the circumstances require it, "I see a _____ and state the object you see. Then adding AND between each thing you see, state 4 other items you see in the surroundings. It might sound like this; "I see a lamp AND I see a rug AND I see a chair AND I see a cup AND I see a desk. Repeating the AND between each observation is important to add to the grounding and slowing down process for the mind.

Then you list five things you hear with AND between each and then move on to five things you feel. The feel is physically, not internally or emotionally. For example, I feel my feet on the carpet AND I feel the breeze on my face, and similar.

It is beneficial in this exercise to stay away from internal feelings such as butterflies in the stomach or sadness. This exercise is meant to ground you in the present space through the senses of sight, hearing and touch. Once you've gone through 5 of each—see, hear and feel physically, you continue with 4 thing as you see hear and feel, then 3 and then 2 and finally one. Always remember the AND in between each. You will find this exercise gives the mind a task to work on and a cooling effect on the anxious body. You can do this wherever you are subtly enough that others don't see it.

As noted earlier, sometimes it's best not to go into the body, so the 5-4-3-2-1 is effective. For example, if on is on the subway feeling panicked or anxious.

When fear is presenting in the body then energy exercises by Donna Eden or the Trauma Sequence or EFT might be more effective. Instructions for these exercised can be found on YouTube - see Endnotes, Resources.

Saying, "I'm breathing in 2-3-4, I'm breathing out 2-3-4, while letting your lower jaw hand and tongue feel heavy and thick, visualizing a blank white room you are in may help to calm soothe and settle your system.

No single method works for everyone, so try out these exercises, modify and combine them in ways that make them yours. Do what helps you the most. Customize to suit your needs. I also suggest practising these exercises when you don't need them will make them more available and helpful in times when you will need them.

Breathe, Ground and Observe

1. Have a notebook and pen handy, close your eyes and become aware of your breath. Notice the point where you shift from an in breath to an out breath. See if you can lengthen each breath in and out ever so slightly. Feel ground under your feet and feel the chair under your pelvis and behind your back. Find ground in these contact points coming up to meet your body. Feel the support of these. Open the body to receive their support. Now feel gravity on your body, the weight of your physical body held to ground through the force of gravity. Imagine your body as an hourglass with the grains of sand flowing down towards the ground settling in your lower limbs.

Now track any sensations that you are aware of in your body at this time: any tension or active energy. Where are they located in your body? Be curious about them without trying to do anything about them at all. Are you aware of any fear in your body right now? If so, where is it? How do you recognize it as fear? Does it change as you observe it? Does it grow larger, move or disappear and hide? If it could speak to you, what would it say? How old were you? When did it first come into being? Where were you? Who was around at the time? If it could tell you whatever it wants to, what would that be? What does it need you to know about why it's there? Does it need to hear from you or what does it need you to do? Be open to hearing whatever it says, without judging. Ask if there is anything else it needs to tell you. Thank it for sharing and let it know that you will be back and want to know more by keeping connected.

Now write down what your experience was like, what you learned and discovered about the fear that you carry in your body.

Once you have finished this writing, share your findings with a friend or the group depending on your situation. I then suggest selecting one or two things you've learned and move with them, dramatize them, develop a character, add a prop or costume piece or create a story line for them. Keep it short and simple. Don't overthink it. It doesn't have to be sophisticated or polished. One body shape, gesture or movement along with the relevant words will do. For example the phrase might be "School was never safe." You begin sitting at an imaginary desk, writing in a notebook, a scary element enters the room, which you could play

136

the action and reaction to. You may run and hide or come out fighting and slay the dragon triumphantly or get slain and die a dramatic death.

Physical

Live and Die

2. Since death is the ultimate scary scenario it is fun to dramatize it. I have people walking around the room eyes looking forward holding others in their periph- eral vision. When someone enters your full vision it's like you've been stabbed and you die, collapsing to the floor. Then you stand up and carry on. Each time you fall, you get stabbed in a different place; a fatal stab to the stomach may be followed by a blow to the head or a shot to the back. It sounds a bit morbid but it gets quite creative and playful while addressing a highly charged fact of life... that we're all going to die one day.

Expression of Fear

I like to use a form of analysis drawn from *Diamond Heart*, a spiritual practice that uses inquiry as a pathway into one's inner world.

Facing each other in pairs, you exchange notebooks or phones, so that one can record for the other their responses to this next inquiry. The respondent may close their eyes if desired. It helps to go deeper in most cases but it's not necessary.

Person A asks the repeating question of person B, "How does your fear express itself?" Person B re- sponds with whatever comes to them, and person A writes it in the respondents' notebook or records it on their phone. She then says "Thank you." And repeats the question, "How does your fear express itself?" and the same process goes on for 7-10 minutes. The repeating question takes the respondent deeper with each repetition of the question. When the time is up, the partners switch.

At the end of the session, each person has their notebook or phone with their recorded answers to the inquiry. They review their answers and see what pops off the page for them. Using this material, they can write for 20 minutes exploring this topic further, or move with it, sound with it, draw it, dramatize it or combine their stories with another in a movement piece or a dramatic rendition of the combination of both of their findings.

If you don't have a partner to work with you could do the inquiry by asking yourself the question, "How does my fear express itself?" pause to find a response and write it down, or record it, then repeat the question once again. It's a bit choppy as you have to come up and out of the process to write or record the answers, but it still works.

A spatial way to work with fear is by establishing a large taped off area in the room in which everyone places their fears on a sheet of paper or in a bundle wrapped up tight with string and paper or strips of cloth then sits around the edges of the taped off area. Exploring one's relationship with the area and the bundle or list of fears can be an improvisation that could go on for up to an hour, if people can sustain that.

"How do I enter the space where my fear is kept and how do I interact with it?" It's surprising what happens for people exploring their relationship with their fears through physical interaction.

When the exercise is finished, people can write or draw their findings on paper with pastels or crayons, and share with others.

Exploring the Inner Critics

This exercise may be done as a group, dyad or as a solo work. Adapt it to your needs.

Begin with an assumption and a discussion of how our negative thoughts come from our inner critics and judges and that they are there to protect us in some way – to keep us safe and out of physical harm and emotional discomfort. Introduce the question, "What do your judges say?" List the critical statements by the judges on a chart.

They might say;

- *I'm not very good*
- *I'll never be Monet*
- *I'm not smart enough*
- *I'm not _____ (fill in the blank) enough.*

Then we respond to the inner critic with, "I know you are trying to be helpful and keep me safe but the way you are doing it isn't helping me. Let's work together to find better ways so that I feel safe and supported."

> *Then explore the question, "What does your inner support system or fan club say to you to cheer you on?" Those statements might include;*
>
> • *Good Job*
>
> • *Well done*
>
> • *Keep going*
>
> • *So brave of you*
>
> • *I love that you did that.*
>
> *Focus on the positive and it expands to fill the space. Take the attention away from the negative and it diminishes, especially when you add, "I know that you're just trying to protect me but this isn't helping me right now. If you encouraged me with a statement such as "I am good enough," or "I can do this," or "Good job!" (said out loud) you would be more helpful and supportive and I would love you for it. Could you try that instead? Thank-you."*

If your frightened parts sense your respect, awareness and growing trust, without judgement, they will reveal more to you creatively. Accepting all that shows up with love and gratitude will promote a deeper, fuller sharing. I know it's often difficult for us, but the less we *'should'* on ourselves, judge, bully, or coerce and the more we encourage and validate, the further we get with our healing and wholeness. That's just the way it is!

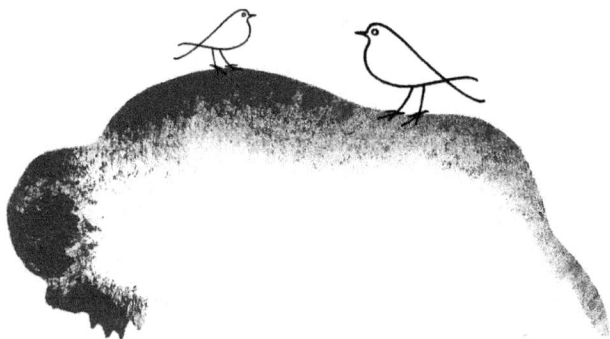

Chapter 8

Creativity and Shame, Blame and Guilt

The Merriam Webster Dictionary defines shame as "a condition of humiliating disgrace or disrepute." A number of different emotions contribute to this condition, such as feelings of unworthiness, inadequacy, humiliation and regret. One might feel embarrassed, disgraced, unclean or disconnected.

I was shamed so much growing up that just writing this list I'm fragmenting a little; my body is tightening, my breath becoming shallower and my mind is beginning to scramble off in all directions. Fortunately, having done all the work I have, as I notice this reaction my response is, "Oh, hello. I can see this is triggering a defence response," and I go into repair mode.

I put down the writing for a moment, place a hand over my heart, one on my forehead and breathe for a few moments to calm, soothe and settle my system. I say to to the activated part, *"I can feel that you're activated by this topic we're writing about so I'm putting my pen down and attending to you. You're important to me. You are safe with me. I love you and won't shame you anymore. I will protect you for others shame. It was wrong that you were shamed growing up. You shouldn't have been. You were just a child. You weren't doing anything wrong. I now lift the burden of that past shame off your small shoulders and give it over to a higher power."* I then make a gesture of lifting a heavy weight off of my chest, or wherever I am aware of it being, raising it up and setting it down. I pause to feel the new lightness. *"You were feeling unsafe but I got you now."* I feel the small smile that touches my lips and I return to my work.

We react to shame by hiding from uncomfortable feelings in order to save face or to support the safety and structure of the self. So shame is a helper/protector trying to keep us safe and intact.

Having said that, shame is also one of the most uncomfortable states there is. At least with fear, we know what it is and can work with it. Shame is difficult to work with in therapy because it hides in the shadows. As a protector its intention is to keep us small and non-threatening so as not to be a visible target. We often feel ashamed that we have shame, so pointing it out reinforces its resolve. Compassion and acceptance offer relief and possible freedom from its vice-grip.

When we feel self-conscious about some perceived inadequacy, shame is there. We don't want others to see our flaws or how badly we feel about ourselves.

As a child I heard, "Shame on you," on a daily basis for anything I did or didn't do that Mom thought I should or shouldn't have. It was her primary disciplinary tool to manipulate and control my behaviour, a precursor to yelling and hitting.

- "Homework done yet?" *Nope.* "Shame on you."

- "Have you washed the steps?" *Nope.* "Shame on you."

- "Dishes?" *Nope.* "Shame on you."

- "Tea towels ironed?" "*Unh unh.* "Shame on you."

- "Not in your pyjamas yet?" *No.* "Shame on you."

I suppose it became over-used, barely noticeable and depleted of meaning. S*emantic satiation* is the psychological term when enough repetition of a word or phrase causes a loss of meaning to a phrase. I was equally threadbare, towing the line, obedient out of a fear of some free-floating threat of violence. My sense of basic goodness and intelligence was suspended in the balance. I had to fight for it daily.

I was apologetic, played small and weak but was seething underneath. That anger needed to be unearthed and expressed.

Later in my life, I was shamed in a movement class taught by a brilliant but brutal teacher. I had just arrived in Toronto from Saskatchewan, new to the big city, coming from a tight-knit dance community in Saskatoon, Saskatchewan. I was a meek and mild-mannered prairie girl, polite, with a slightly nervous disposition. She was a strict authoritarian who believed in the strip-down build-up method of teaching.

Mid-way through one of her classes she demonstrated a sequence of movements and told us to repeat it. Then asked us to repeat it again. Tension was mounting in the room. Half way through the second sequence she shouted, "*Tuk!"* Something that we knew meant "Stop!"

Startled by the tone of her command we jerked and lurched to a stop, bumping into one another in a film noir version of the Three Stooges.

She said, *"You!"* and thrust a gnarly index finger directly at my face from across the room. *"Do zee move."*

Shocked by the request and with no apparent escape, I repeated the move as best I could under close scrutiny from her and the other dancers who were watching me in horror, relieved it wasn't them.

Then she continued, *"Ya, do zee move again!"*

I repeated the sequence much worse this time due to escalating nerves. At that point she threw her arms up in the air and exclaimed in an aggressive, exasperated tone, *"Ya! Zat's how NOT to do zee move!"*

I crumbled on the spot. Deconstructing from the inside. Yet, in spite of my condition, I continued the class, sniffling, wiping, choking back the tears right to the finish.

I don't know how or why I kept going—I couldn't breathe. My body had gone stiff. I struggled to move. Shame and humiliation gripped me like a suit of armour, killing any pleasure I might have had. I just wanted to disappear.

Other class members stole tentative glances at me from the side with attempts at conveying empathy and support.

As the class wrapped up, this teacher came over, looked me straight in the eye, inches away from my face, gripped my shoulders firmly with her hands and said, *"Ya, you good student. I vork vith you."* Then she turned and walked away.

Was that supposed to make me feel better? A line from theatre comes to mind, *"Lacerated by my last human encounter, I stagger on to the next."* Had I passed some test required to work with her? Was it meant to weed out the weak?

Another of her favorite lines was, *"No! You do ZAT, you make your boody zick!"*

I left the class and didn't return. It wasn't a fit for me. I knew enough to quit while I was ahead. Many continued to study with her for years after that, forever in fear and awe of her.

Dance in those days could be a world where only the strong survived. I once had the back of my thigh bitten by a male modern dance instructor at York for not lifting my leg high enough—insane behaviour for any teacher.

I taught for many years in a style that was dramatically different from those abusive instructors. I worked from an approach that was gentler, yet still challenging. It was supportive, positive and encouraging. There was no room for public humiliation, teacher to student or student to student. Those were my rules.

Years later I performed in The Dance Goes On at the *Du-Maurier Theatre*, Harbourfront Centre, Toronto. The show was for choreographers over the age of 40. Karen Kain, Danny Grossman and other big names were on the program. I and a small group of fellow dancers joined forces to create a clown performance built from our collective traumatic experiences received at the hands of a number of dance teachers we had studied with.

The piece we did was a clown performance with a very strict ballet mistress toting a switch that cracked and popped balloons that we had stuffed in our ballet tights. This character spat out phrases such as, '*You are too fat. Shoulders back. Chest out. Belly in. Head up. What are you doing in dance, you should be a plumber! Everyone must struggle and suffer!*'

As I reflect on my exposure to toxic dance instructors, I realize it could have been much worse. I could have been so humiliated and shamed by these people that I gave up dance altogether. Luckily I had a solid base of positive dance experiences, nurtured by a number of previous kinder, gentler teachers, that this didn't break my passion for dance.

I've heard traumatic stories in my therapy practice of individuals who have had long standing passions painfully wiped out by one humiliating boss or teacher in a single traumatic event or series of events. It's unfortunate that people in positions of power hurt others.

Some teachers believe that this approach "toughens you up" and readies you for the harsh world of competitive dance or theatre. It's an Old School attitude; "I survived it, so I have a right to pass it on."

In my opinion nothing positive comes from this type of approach, any more than it does out of spanking or yelling at a child. The child may cooperate in the moment out of fear, but the injury remains and will influence future relationships and events one way or another.

The lack of self-compassion and acceptance felt by a shamed person gets projected onto others. In the fairy tale Snow White, the Evil Queen asks the mirror in her room, "Mirror, mirror on the wall, who's the fairest of them all?" As long as the mirror answers, "You are the fairest in the land," to the queen, all is well. But as soon as the mirror answers, "Snow White," the queen plots to have her murdered.

I often find clients need to get in touch with their anger in order to heal the shame they have taken on from those who shamed them in the past. They are then able to get free of both the anger and shame they carry.

We may internalize this injury, feeling that we should be doing something better or more effectively than we are. We may have unrealistic expectations of ourselves and live on a tight rope of fear that people will see just how flawed, stupid, or unacceptable we are.

Failure to meet our internal expectations, ideals or standards creates a state of possible self-hatred where we want to hide or withdraw from others. It is a debilitating state. We may turn to addiction to manage toxic shame.

In couples work I often witness one partner who responds to any feedback or discontent from the other partner by sinking into their own devouring shame. They shut down and withdraw from the partner who is trying to reach out and connect with them to improve their relationship.

Uncovering shame and working with it in safe and compassionate ways supports the health and vitality of our creativity and relationships. I have included exercises at the end of this chapter that can assist in building awareness and repairing the self from negative effects caused by shame.

Blame and Guilt

Shame has to do with who you have been taught to believe you are, or who you think or feel or experience yourself to be. Blame focuses the fault for how you think or feel projected out onto other individuals or groups who you believe to be responsible for your present condition.

Often evaluation of the source of these current beliefs, the past actions by those responsible and the associated feelings need to be addressed before one can move on. These stances may go back deep into childhood, but are now holding the person hostage. That person is unable to connect or find the love and support they most desire. A state of blame is a powerless state. It is often fuelled by anger, and yet it is a very stuck and often very insecure position underneath.

I often sit with couples where one partner is angry at the other, blaming them for "never listening." In response, the other partner shuts down and withdraws behind a wall. In this situation I point out that all conflict between couples is an attempt to connect.

Then I slow things down and say to the blaming partner, "It sounds like you don't feel seen or heard by your partner right now and it's frustrating for you. It's important to you that he gets it because he's important to you. Well I'm here to help with that. I can see you, hear you and even witness your feelings right now and maybe help him do the same. What do you need him to know right now? If he could take it in?"

Then the anger softens; sadness, fear and other vulnerable feelings arise and the withdrawn partner often drops the defensive stance and reaches out with comfort, which is what the first partner wanted to begin with. In this way, the couple are able to close the gap between them.

In our house we employ humour to deal with the situation when blame might show up because the milk has been left on the counter or a tap left running in the bathroom. We start a light-hearted banter back and forth:

"It wasn't me."

"I didn't do it."

"I wasn't even there."

"Must have been the cat."

In sessions, I'll delve into guilt and blame with creative ways to identify and work with couples creatively in order to release the grip these states have on us, our relationships, and our creativity by playing with and through them.

Someone with shame doesn't feel like they are a good enough person to be able to do anything about the situation they find themselves in. A guilty person can do something about it and then move past it. Toxic guilt usually has shame embedded within it and often leaves someone feeling helpless and bad about themselves.

Healthy guilt is guilt that we feel when we have inadvertently or deliberately hurt someone with our words or actions. A repair is needed, where we own up to what we've done, recognize the impact it's had on the other person, feel genuine remorse, and apologize for our actions that have hurt the other person.

I see more *toxic* guilt than healthy guilt in individuals or in couple's relationships. For example an individual may feel guilt from their parent's divorce or their abuse or abandonment, none of which was their fault. It wasn't anything they could have influenced since they were only a child at the time and not responsible for any of it. Yet they carry a burden of guilt around with them throughout their childhood and adult years. It comes into their relationships and affects their access to happiness.

Holding the innocence as you explore the following exercises into gentle inquiry and exploration of shame and guilt will take you the furthest. Give yourself permission to slow or pause when needed.

Chapter 8 Exploration of Shame

Physical Warm Up - Tense and Release

Tensing and releasing muscles, as described in the previous chapter, is a good way to begin. Take a body part, an arm for example and tense the muscles holding for the count of 5 or 6 seconds then release. Move on to the other arm, then each leg and the belly, pelvis, face, scalp, neck, jaw, shoulders, back, butt, continuing until you've covered the whole body. Then tense areas of the body, the upper, lower, front and back then tense the whole body for a few seconds and release it. Holding and releasing the breath, along with your muscles, enhances the effect.

Movement

Gravity Inquiry — Hall of Shame

Shame has weight to it so feel into gravity by lifting one arm then letting it drop to your side, then the other arm. While standing, lift a leg and hold it under the knee then let it drop being careful not to have it hit the floor too hard. Repeat with the other leg.

Now droop your shoulders protecting your heart and cover your face as you drop your head and take a walk through the hall of shame. See all the times and places and people where you felt shamed. Pause to record in your journal as you go. Where in your body do you carry your shame?

Physical Theatre - Group Shame

As a band of outcasts, huddle together and travel through the room hiding and protecting yourselves from outside danger. Feel the unsafe environment around you. Find twisted, gnarled, shapes in the body and travel, head down in fear, disgrace and shame. Put on tattered clothes and make your face dirty. Find a tic that you have that you're trying to hide. It might be belching or farting or a twitch or a sound that escapes from you uncontrollably that you must hide or feel humiliated for having it and letting it show. As an instructor with actors I would beat a drum to represent the danger taunting the group with words like, shame on you while tsk-ing and frowning to further embarrass them. Perform an unsightly, loathsome, not-fit-to-be-seen gesture or sound then feel the shame of it being seen.

Pair up and play roles with each other, one in a shameful gesture or action with the other judging and shaming the, showing disgust. Then switch roles. Have fun with it. Let it grow to the absurd. This is freeing to explore as all of us have parts that we fear being seen by others. Pause to share your findings. Then write about any part of this that stays with you for 30 minutes and share again.

The Sounds of Shame

> *What are the sounds that shame makes? Begin by becoming aware of your breath. Then gently touch sound on an exhale with a sigh that slightly activates the vocal cords. Repeat that sound. Find further sounds that express the weight in the body that you explored earlier. What sounds come with a drooping head and shoulders? What sounds are you making behind the hands that cover your face? The sounds of your shame that get expressed when no one is watching? Remember, there are no mistakes, no wrong answers and if there are no sounds let that be OK as well. Try a silent scream like Edvard Munch's painting of The Scream. Then hide.*

Writing

Expressions of Shame

> *Ask a repeating question, "How does my shame express itself?" either alone or with a partner and record the responses. Say thank you and then ask the question again. Continue for 7-10 minutes then reflect on your responses taking what pops off the page into a further write or create a poem on shame.*

On the next two pages is a personal response written from my own raw experience of shame.

Shame on Me

A sliver the size of my body
sits festering underneath my skin.
I pick away at it. It bleeds and hurts like hell.
I back away for a bit of healing time then go at it again.
I shouldn't have it. It's wrong.
And I certainly I shouldn't admit to having it.
Or be writing about it right now.
Letting everyone and their dog see the damn thing
Me with it and digging at it.
Shame on me.
Disgusting for sure. Go away.
What's wrong with you?
Leave it well enough alone.
You'll make yourself sick if you keep this up.
This is inappropriate. You need to stop.

My cat leans in, pressing his head firmly to my lips.
I take a long, deliberate inhale of his earthy scent
Through a nose that's buried deep in his fur
We're both sniffers
He knows my scent and my bottomless pit.
He doesn't back away from it.
We press into each other each day for comfort and safety,

Falling asleep for short cat-naps on the couch
between periods of work.

An inner critic pipes up, "OMG that's just pathetic,
hide all of that will you ... it's ... well, pathetic."
Walls of internal storage bins house a lifetime of
embarrassments.
Injuries incurred from too much of this
and not enough of that.

An exhausted soul pushes a wheel barrel of bones,
brittle from abuse, abandonment, neglect.
Pressing in on itself
Like a home-made bomb ready to blow,
A grenade of emotion, the pin begging to be pulled,
Be released, disarmed, free at last, landing
finally in tiny particles,
Rejoicing the earth, harmless, hidden once again
Safe for now anyway.

~Audrey C. Jolly

Visual Art

Collage of Shame

1. Collage from magazines images depicting shame for you.

2. Draw heavy, dark lines and shapes. Draw with light colours then cover over with black crayon. Scratch away the black revealing the light underneath it.

Share your findings with a partner – your art, writing or movement and then combine them in new ways. Possibly your partner moves the shapes or colours of your drawing, or adds a soundscape to your movements or one person's writing is lifted off the page and improvised using movement and sound then shaped into a repeatable movement study. The possibilities are endless. Let your imagination play with the possibilities and unfold as it will.

Writing

Accuser and the Accused

1. Write about a time when you were blamed for something, correctly or falsely. Take 20 minutes to do this. Then write about a time when you blamed someone for something, correctly or falsely.

With a partner assign have one person be the accuser and the other the accused. You can do this theatre improv in gibberish or in English. Use a line such as "You hit my car," or "That's my bike you're riding, you stole my bike," or any line you decide on. The stakes can go up with, "That's my child. You stole my child." Feel into the accuser role and the accused role. In the accused role do you retaliate with aggression or cower in guilt and shame? Or do you blame the accuser who is blaming you? Try all three positions. Get creative, play with it. See how the dynamic shifts when you are actually at fault for what you are accused of or being falsely accused of something you didn't do.

The length of the improv may be 7 to 20 minutes or longer. Once the improv is done, shift to writing about the experiences or have paper and pastels available to draw the experiences or have a space you can move in and embody the experience of it, non-verbally.

2. A follow-up segment could be a movement exploration where each person finds gestures or positions in the body that capture their experience. Take three of these gestures or positions and link them together to form a movement sequence adding a movement which takes them from one position to the next. Choose a beginning and end position. Think of high, medium and low-level options, i.e.: standing, kneeling, lying when you make your choices. Share this sequence with your partner.

Now choose potent words from your writing to insert into your movement study playing around with the words, drawing them out slowly like you're chewing toffee or punching them out like a boxer or whispering them out or shaking as you speak. Share this combined voice, text and movement study with your partner.

If you are really keen with the time and energy for it, you can blend the partners studies into a combined voice and movement study. Then share these studies

with the larger group and share the experiences after-
wards.

If this feel overly complex, as it may to the non-actor,
then just take a piece of it to work with. Some part of
it that feels manageable and let the rest of it go for
now. Don't judge yourself for it.

This could shift into visual art and further writing if
you are working over a longer period of time with built
in breaks. You and your partner might reverse roles.

As you can see, there are repeating patterns that weave
through each theme involving a variety of art forms—each
one building on the last. Over time you will hopefully be
able to mix, match and choose what's best for you.

Always end with gratitude to the self for this delicate inquiry into often difficult inner terrain. Seek support if you
need it.

Chapter 9

Creativity and Sorrow

I define sorrow as a deep sense of distress, disappointment and loss. All of us experience sorrow in our lives. Sorrow can be felt with the loss of a loved one or a pet or job or a home, as a natural response to events occurring in the present.

Sadness is a state of unhappiness and is a basic human emotion. Sorrow is a more intense form of sadness. Grief is an even more intense reaction to a greater sense of loss and often stays around for a longer period of time.

Everyone deals with loss and expresses their sadness, sorrow and grief differently. For the purpose of this work let us identify sadness as a small response, sorrow a medium one and grief a large response to some loss or disappointment.

Sorrow may also be carried in the body often without an understanding of what, where, when or why it's there. For example, without a person knowing it, they might be carrying childhood sorrow from not receiving love or connection. That person then searches the world over looking for the love they didn't get; this affects all the relationships they enter as adults and may lead to addiction, attempting to soothe and mask uncomfortable, feelings.

We so often resist feeling sorrow, whether it be present or from the past. It gets stored and blocked in the body and causes a host of issues on many levels. It's an emotion that we tend to dread and avoid at all cost. But there is a cost to that avoidance. It takes energy and emotional effort to avoid sorrow that could be met, released and the energy be put to better use. Collapsing into a puddle in the arms of a safe, loving person with all your sorrow pouring out to be witnessed and held is very healing. We fear dissolving or being overtaken completely with our sorrow but for the majority of people it's only another fear that is getting stacked on top of the sorrow; one emotion, sorrow, gets hijacked by another emotion, fear.

Giving ourselves permission to grieve and receive emotional comfort in a safe container is such an important part of becoming whole. I can't stress it enough. Repairing the damage done to our grief-stricken parts is critical to our health and wellbeing.

I had a therapist say to me once, *"It's only grief — feeling nothing would be worse."* I don't necessarily agree with her approach, nor would I handle the moment the same way as a therapist, but I do get the point she was making... getting in touch with grief won't kill you, even if it feels like it might.

I've witnessed many moments where the loss of a child or partner was being explored, processed and released through cleansing tears. I have personally wept in *Authentic Movement* sessions where I was lovingly witnessed and held by others as I connected with past grief held in the body over my lifetime. This early childhood grief could not

162

be unearthed through talking alone as it was pre-cognitive and pre-verbal yet it influenced my life in dramatic ways, depression being one of them. Much of my art, consciously or unconsciously has been an attempt to heal deep grief caused by abandonment by those who should have kept me safe and feeling supported.

Much of the therapy I do is helping people build a tolerance for their feelings. When feelings and sensations in the body become too much and intolerable to hold, we resort to our defences to manage them. Dropping fully into sorrow is difficult for the majority of people. It feels as though it could swallow you up and drag you out to sea.

There is a great deal of fear associated with experiencing sorrow. Sorrow can trigger our fears of loss and death. We avoid it, but it's only a feeling. When met fully and held by a strong, loving self, these feelings can be embraced and expressed. Having a good cry can be very healing if you can stay present for it and allow it. If you find yourself exhausted or getting lost in your sorrow, unable to function, you may need help with it to prevent depression.

I recall being in Greece at a friend's mother's funeral where the son walked behind the cart carrying his mother's body through the coastal town towards the gravesite. He walked between two of his male friends, howling and wailing to the gods with gut-wrenching grief. The whole town was witness to his agony and pain. Periodically he crumpled to the ground in a heap of anguish and despair, and his two friends then picked him up. As the polite, repressed Canadian that I was, I found it all a bit surreal, as though I was in some theatrical Greek tragedy. His culture was able to express their grief in ways that I had never seen before.

Wailing mourners trailed the procession—a choir of elderly women, townspeople and friends of the family.

I have never forgotten that experience. I know from my own experience that it can feel good to wail loudly and passionately, soaking a therapist's shirt with my tears. I believe we don't give ourselves permission to express sorrow enough in our culture.

Working with blocks to sorrow is much the same as working with blocks to other feelings. We may find we have judgements about our sorrow; perhaps our inner critics believe it is weak to 'break down and cry.' I certainly got that message growing up. "Stop crying like a baby" was a shaming statement I heard as a child. It sucked all the air out of my sails leaving a feeling of isolation and powerlessness in a moment when I was already feeling vulnerable and in need of comfort and love. Repairing wounds like that takes time.

Blocks to sorrow can be worked with creatively, physically, energetically, and intellectually. They are then allowed to ease up on their role to protect and our grief can be accessed. Emotional safety and comfort is the key to the success of this. A collective howling at the moon — the way wolves or coyotes or even dogs do—can be cathartic and feel good. Actors *fake it till they make it* for stage performance.

A laugh is very close to a cry, so laughing until you're crying is relatively easy to set up. I used to have actors lie down with their head on another's belly in a circle then tell them "whatever you do, don't laugh." Then someone would inevitably start to giggle, and a wave or series of waves of laughter would ring out contagiously until people were crying with laughter, their sides sore from the muscles releasing and everyone in a puddle of expressed emotion. It's a good thing to have sorrow in your theatre tool kit as inevitably one needs to play a grieving widow or friend at some point and knowing how to get there while looking genuine is essential.

In Halifax I was observing a run of a play where the late Maxim Mazumdar shed a tear on the same line of a play every night for a week. I felt that he was delivering certain emotion laden lines directly to me. I felt a bit uncomfortable with the intimacy of it and then realized, looking around that others felt the very same way, both men and women alike. Impressive acting skills!

In my teaching days in theatre, often a specific movement or character or scene in a play has triggered sorrow or grief for an actor. All too often others rush in to soothe and distract the person away from their feelings believing they are doing them a favour. But grief needs space and time and witnessing with compassion rather than intervention. Doing less is more in the face of someone's sorrow. Being present with the person's grief is enough; trying to fix it or talk the person out of the discomfort of it robs them of their experience. I've heard people say, "You don't have to cry." Well, they obviously do!

Grief and sorrow are a part of life not to be avoided. Some years ago, I was at my cousin's home in Regina when mom was dying of cancer in a local hospital. During grace I began to break down and cry because my mom was not able to be with us and would soon be gone forever. A cousin, sitting beside me, gave me a swift elbow to the ribs and said, "Buck up kid." At which point I sucked up my grief and swallowed it for the duration of the meal and evening. I could barely eat or breathe but that's how my family dealt with our grief—we sucked it up and sojourned on. Good farm stock Saskatchewan people, who had their share of

165

hardship, meant well, were loving and supportive in their own way, but emotionally repressed.

You don't have to do anything for someone in grief other than being there, preferably not in pity or sympathy but a neutral open-hearted presence. Asking if they would like touch – a hug, for instance — is one thing, but assuming they would and imposing it on them may take them away from their feelings. I've learned to sit attentively and allow what needs to be revealed to come forward.

Each person decides for themselves what their path through grief will be, always mindful of the capacity it has to cause debilitating depression.

Creativity works best in relation to past sorrow as a way of finding it, exploring it creatively and transforming it by having a reparative experience where thoughts and feelings are released and witnessed, where one feels seen and met, safe and cared for. Those sorrowful parts of the self get to come into the world and be reunited with the self and finally feel a part of the whole rather than abandoned or 'exiled' as Richard Schwartz names it in Internal Family Systems Therapy. Those parts get to put down the burden of sorrow they may have carried for a lifetime of feeling unloved or unwanted.

Sadness, sorrow or grief might be felt in response to a current loss or in response to some past event or loss. These get processed differently. One is present time and the other is uncovering stored feelings from the past. One is immediate and understandable; past grief may not have the same understandable aspect,but it is no less significant and important to attend to.

Early childhood grief and loss can run our adult decision-making and relationships in dramatic ways. We need to resolve these if we want to live with full vitality in healthy, rewarding relationships.

Being rocked and sung a lullaby while crying like a baby can be healing when the time is right. Even making up for traumatic in-utero experiences in safe loving arms can be life giving. Grief can be met physically, emotionally, energetically and spiritually. But first we have to reach the grief, which may not be easy.

We all carry pockets of grief that surface at times when the circumstances activate it. People have specific movies that trigger their grief every time they watch it or a song or poem. Allow these expressions to breathe, move and release. Here are some supportive ways to explore these delicate feelings.

Chapter 9 Exercises in Sorrow

Language

Expressions of Sorrow

> *Asking the repeating questions, either alone or with a partner, "How does your sorrow express itself? Where in your body do you carry Sorrow?" [Sorrow may be replaced with sadness or grief for the purpose of this exercise.]*
>
> *A writing prompt might be, "I'm afraid to feel my sorrow because _____"*

Visual Art

Body Mapping

> *Lie down on a large piece of paper and have a partner trace an outline of your body. Then using coloured pastels or paint draw your sorrow, where and how you experience it. [As with the above exercise, sorrow may be interchanged with sadness or grief. See how this might affect your results.]*
>
> *Pick three colours for sorrow and do a series of drawings or paintings from the part of you that holds your sorrow and sadness. Let it pour out not from the head but from the body. Your non-dominant hand may be used for this. Don't think about it.*

Movement and Sound

Physical Warm Up - Tension and Release

A good physical warm up for this creative work with sorrow is 'tense and release' muscle work, 'described in Chapter 7.

Ice to Vapour

> *Ice to vapour is a movement improv that can expand to include vocal work where the mover begins in an image of their body as a block of ice. It's important to become the image and not feel as though you are a human being subjected to the images. There is no pain or suffering to any of this. As the ice is heated up, your body as the block of ice, begins to melt and become more fluid. Let this melting inform your shapes and body movements. As more imaginary heat is added begin to transition into a boiling, bubbling water like a*

168

pot on the stove - not reacting negatively, but playing as the bubbling water until you evaporate into the air as steam - floating away into the air. You will have transitioned from the qualities of earth to water to fire and air. Feeling the contrasting qualities as you go. Then you can repeat the exercise using vocal sound only then a third time combining both movement and sound. Skip the vocal only if it feels too difficult to do, go as far as you can with this and stop when you need to. Be satisfied with your results for now.

Vocally, you can begin with the breath transitioning to a tiny whimper to a louder vocal complaint, building to a wail. In twos, one person van be the comforter of the whimpering to wailing child, then receive the comfort returning back through the transitions to whimpering and silence.

Body Shapes

Find three body shapes for your sorrow and move between them, possibly at a low, medium and high level. Share them with a friend who may then accompany you with an instrument or sounds they make. What are the rhythm and timing (fast/slow) of your sorrow? Moan and wail and howl and whine. Give in to gravity and collapse to the floor dissolve into a puddle, flow like a river. Turn in, gather up your sorrow and pour it out through your heart and soul and spirit. Meet it fully and honour and release it.

Remember to establish a safe container for yourself with someone to support you as you delve into these vulnerable, sometimes raw feeling places.

Sorrow Inquiry Through the Elements

As a warm up, curl your body into a small ball on the floor. Feel into the weight of your body. Feel gravity weighing heavily on you. Slow down your breath and feel the burden of sorrow and grief that you're carrying. Where in your body do you feel it? Place your hand over that area. Now slowly rise to standing feeling the weight of grief in your body and walk slowly through the room with it.

Lift an arm and let it drop then lift the other arm and do the same. If you have a partner to work with have them lift one of your arms giving over the weight of it then letting it drop to your side. Have your partner take the weight of your head and hold it as you slowly droop to the floor into a position of lying on your back. Then rolling to one side come back up to standing giving the weight of your head over to the hands of your partner as best you can.

Take a walk through the space standing upright then feel the weight of gravity increasing on your body until you hunch over and feel heavier and heavier. Feel into exhaustion carrying this excess weight on your shoulders and in the body. Feel the weight of the world on your shoulders. If you have lots of big pillows or large sports balls you can add actual physical weight to your body or have a partner weigh you down by pressing their arms on your shoulders or hang onto your ankle as you try to walk dragging the weight behind you. Feel the burden.

Having been in the element of earth for this first section of play, now move into the element of water and find flow and fluidity in the quality of your movements.

170

Be a dripping tap progressing to a running tap to a torrential rain storm and a Force 10 typhoon or tornado. Return to the mid-range of your exploration of water and move with comfortable fluidity with loose joints and continuous movement. It doesn't have to be big movement it might be in one arm with the image of sea grasses being moved by wave action of the water around it while rooted in the sea floor.

Now explore weight and water together moving back and forth between them, being heavy and weighed down with a huge burden on your shoulders. Then collapse into water and flow at whatever intensity feels right for you, a drop or a river. Now let the muscles of your face droop as in a pout with a tear of sadness and a small, whimpering sound while feeling more weight and allow yourself to explore a drop of grief through to an over the top wail still in weight and water. Remember "fake it 'til you make it." This funny phrase is useful, in the beginning, because we are wired to respond emotionally when enacting certain postures and actions, even mechanically. It's OK if it's 'acted' and not authentic sorrow and grief, especially in the beginning. Sketch it in and see where you get— always returning to weight and water for your baseline.

Once you're done, record your findings on paper through writing or drawing then share them with a partner or the group. What did you find? Where in your body do you hold your grief? What blocks did you meet along the way? What judges or critics?

Thank yourself for showing up for these explorations. Take luxurious bah or shower, drink water, refill and renew.

Chapter 10

Creativity and Joy

I recall being at a couple's retreat, sitting at the dinner table where couples laughed and chatted together and I was struck by the amount of love in the room. I had a profound body and nervous system sensation, an inner fireworks display of positive energy and I thought, "Oh, so this is what happiness feels like." What had been foreign to me, especially in relationship to others, was now unmistakably present. I had a feeling of 'coming home' to something beyond what my family home had been able to provide for me in terms of safety, acceptance and love. A feeling of deep gratitude followed this moment.

Much of the time in therapy is spent working with our pain and suffering, not on our joy. Difficult thoughts, feelings and sensations, plus the blocks we have constructed around them, need to be heard, felt, expressed and repaired. But what do we do all of this for? We do this work in order to free ourselves for a more positive, expansive life experience, one with less contraction and fear. One with more joy and happiness.

As a species, we focus much more on uncomfortable feelings than on the comfortable, pleasant sensations due to our survival instinct. There may come a time when a client arrives at a session and says they are feeling good and don't have anything to work on today in therapy. It's an unfamiliar feeling place for many people.

When this happens, I suggest that we can end the session early or we can explore this new feeling place where they are stress-free, relaxed and happy. We need to devote time and attention to those moments when we are feeling happy, peaceful, calm and safe, especially if these states are less familiar to us than the uncomfortable states. So using a session to explore how one knows they are feeling happy and calm is a worthwhile use of time. It can be explored and embodied more consciously.

When I experience a positive feeling state of any kind and become aware of it I tap in the joy, an energy medicine exercise by Donna Eden where I tap my forehead between my eyebrows and name the feeling I'm in. I might say, "I'm feeling so grateful for the love of my partner right now; my body is vibrating with love." And I usually follow that up with an invitation such as "I am deeply grateful for this feeling and am open and receptive to more of this energy and good feeling knowing that I deserve it."

Keeping in mind that we are clearing the path for our peace and happiness gives a meaning and momentum, which supports the difficult work we must do to get there. Defining what our happiness, peace and satisfaction looks and feels like, as it's unique to each of us, is a valuable, ongoing practice. It will shift as we grow and change, what makes us happy this year or month or week may be different the next. When we define the ways that we block our happiness we can begin to embrace the patterns and shift out of their ruts creating new pathways to our goals.

Creatively exploring and expressing the pleasurable feelings through art and movement can greatly enhance the return and expansion of these states of joy and happiness through focusing on strengths and on the positive. In theatre I ask the class to share what they liked about a fellow classmate's performance and not what didn't work or where it needed improvement. When the performer heard all the feedback about what was already strong in their piece they repeated those strengths in the performance, capitalizing on the feedback. Inevitably more of what worked accrued in their piece and there was less room for what didn't work.

If we capitalize on what makes us happy and we get very clear on how and what and who and where this occurs, we can then fill our lives with more of what makes us happy and less of what is stressful even though it may be the more familiar state. Happiness isn't a given but an awareness and daily practice that involves gratitude and conscious choice. We can shape and create a life that has more satisfaction, joy and pleasure if we approach it with a conscious awareness. Creativity can support this process beautifully.

Chapter 10 Creativity and Joy

Physical Inquiry into Joy

Where in your body do you feel it when you are in a state of joy or happiness? What colour depicts this feeling, what scents, what sounds, what textures? What words come to mind for you? Can you create a short poem from these words or find a posture or movement that expresses this state because inevitably it will not be permanent. When this state is gone and you are suffering or scared or lost recalling this state through any of the means named is a beneficial resource to have.

175

Take the colours and forms and textures that you associate with these positive qualities and make art from them, collages or paintings or drawings or sculpture so that you surround yourself with the reminder of this state for when you feel lost to it. Art can trigger a positive memory in the body and support you in stressful moments when these feelings are out of reach.

Embody Joy

What image depicts pure joy for you? If we want to be a figure skater just trying on some skates and finding some ice with a friend to hold us up while we slide around is a valuable exercise. In the same spirit of experimentation, trying on states of freedom, joy and peace if only for a contrived second through creative play is a valuable exercise.

1. In theatre, students "fake it till they make it" all the time. They "hang out in the ball park" of the feeling they need to embody; if it's joy they try on bubbly, light, quick actions like a pot of popcorn with sound effects or a funny walk or goofy, non-language gibberish. A scene in gibberish might be that you are being told a joke by your friend that causes you to laugh hysterically until your sides split and you fall to the floor rolling with laughter ... Try taking your expression of joy through the roof.

2. Two people competing to top each other by saying only, "I love you" can reach dramatic heights of joy and laughter. Activating the muscles of the heart and/or the gut can be helpful in finding joy and laughter. A 'ha ha' sound that moves the belly or an 'O' sound that resonates in the chest area of the heart then a lower sound that does the same for the belly will also activate energy. Standing facing a partner with the right hand resting on their chest over their heart and the left hand placed on top of their hand that is on your heart, looking into each others' eyes, seeing and being seen deeply can bring up joy. It might also bring up other feelings that can be acknowledged along the way. You could also stand behind a partner and place a hand on their lower back, or back heart area, sending positive energy into their body through your touch. The receiver of the touch can breathe into the contact point then begin to move around the room from that point. Sounding from that place in the body can also be added.

3. Action/response with partners also activates joy. One person makes a sound and movement that takes them through the room: e.g. skips and whistles.) Keep the distance short, in the beginning. The partner then repeats the first person's sound and movement while joining them in the room. Then the second person takes the lead and travels out into the room with a new movement and sound, which the other person will repeat while joining in. It switches back and forth on leader/follower allowing the actions and sounds to become larger, funnier and more animated as inhibitions lift.

Having a regular practice that establishes what you long for and what your current reality is, along with knowledge of what is preventing or holding you back from having this in the present is useful to know. Being curious with all aspects of this balance and inquiring into the desires and fears moves us towards our goals.

Movement

Massage, Shake and Move

Lightly massage the muscles of your feet, calves, thighs and arms, shoulders and neck. Tap over your torso front and back as far as you can reach. If you have a partner in this exercise, tap each other's backs and heads lightly. Run your hands down the body from the head to feet a few times. If this feels challenging for either person, do it just off the edges of the body combing the energy field around the body. Stand in the waterfall of energy feeling the sensations it brings.

Now let your body shake in whatever ways it wants to. Visualize a dog shaking off water after running through a sprinkler on a hot day. Add a panting breath, visualizing a long tongue that hangs to the ground. It's a happy dog. Take a skip around the room with a bounce in your step.

Move joy into your body discovering the shapes, movements and sounds that best express it, then share it with your partner. Blend your movements together into a happy dance and present it to the group.

Writing

Do this repeating questions exercise, either alone or with a partner and a notebook. The questions might be "What brings you joy? How does your joy express itself? How do you know when you are happy?

Then take these findings and create a poem for your joy, one that you can repeat. Share it with a partner.

Free associate with the word 'joy' for other words that come to mind: e.g. elation, happiness or ecstasy. Find associations with song lyrics, poems or prose, and record them. Then blend them into a piece of writing for yourself or a song, which is just a made-up melody added to the words. I would have actors sing what they had for breakfast that morning. Try to put any of this text or writing to a made-up melody.

This exercise may challenge the boundaries of your inhibition-- but that's not a bad thing as long as you feel supported and surrounded by others taking the same creative risks. It leads to more freedom and spontaneity – two conditions that contribute to joy. Building the inner relationships that allow and support more freedom of expression with less inhibition are important. This takes us back to the chapter on fear and how to embrace it.

Visual Art

Expressions of Joy

Using pastels or paint find colours your joy and happiness. Capture the shapes you have explored in your body and the moves that you've found using the art materials at hand. Close your eyes to make it easier to recall them in your body. Then move the text once again incorporating what you have discovered through your art. Share it again and celebrate your findings.

Collaging from magazines or sculpting with clay can also be used to further explore your connection with joy and happiness.

Exploring joy is often seen as less important than healing fear or grief, but joy is as important to cultivate and explore as any other emotion. What thoughts, feelings and sensation in the body accompany the states of joy and happiness? How do they differ from a state of peace or freedom? This is a worthwhile exploration. These experiences are often less common, and we benefit by having them become second nature and more familiar.

Chapter 11

Creativity and Wholeness

To see a World in a Grain of Sand

And a Heaven in a Wild Flower

Hold Infinity in the palm of your hand

And Eternity in an hour.

~ William Blake

This book began with a desire to gather many experiences I had had in life into one basket and hold them as a whole rather than holding them separately inside myself. This need to gather and connect the dots has led to my life's path and this book. It initiated my healing journey and has lead to my careers an artist, educator and psychotherapist. Creativity and emotional work have been the vehicles of transformation for me and many of my students and clients.

Ultimately on my journey, I was in search of a feeling of wholeness that hadn't been available to me while I was growing up. Many experiences had shattered that feeling, right from in the womb where a death in the family and it's impact on my mother dramatically altered my earliest experiences of connection and safety.

I had a lot of work to do to find that sense of 'whole' again. A variety of therapies offered by gifted psychotherapists helped me to do this. I am forever grateful to them. I gathered up a number of extraordinary events that I had experienced during my creative work, reflecting on them as a whole.

These lost parts long to be gathered up and brought home to the self. They wait patiently, or sometimes not so patiently, for us to come and rescue them from their isolation. Creativity and play can reveal these lost parts so that we can identify and retrieve them. They no longer want be saddled with their burdens, but to receive comfort, security, acceptance, warmth, and love, as all healthy, growing children want and need.

It's never too late to free these inner parts, help them to mature and build an inner harmony within the parts.

But at what point in our creative healing process are we ready and able to hold the whole self with compassion, acceptance and love? How do we recognize when we're on the right path? How do we identify and integrate enough aspects of ourselves to give us a feeling of wholeness? When and how do we reach a state of self-love and a sense of 'mystery solved?'

Good questions. None of these states of equilibrium happen overnight.

Internal Family Systems therapy (IFS) is an approach to healing that is built on the idea of internal parts needing our help. We create a sense of integration and wholeness by connecting with lost and traumatized parts of the self, en-

184

couraging an unburdening of the feelings and experiences these parts have carried, some for a very long time.

They carry these intolerable feelings for us so that we can function in other parts of our lives as well as we do. They act as storage bins for our traumatized parts, keeping them away from us so that we can work, fall in love and navigate our lives as effectively as we do.

These parts deserve our sincere gratitude for the way they carry and store these painful experiences for us; otherwise, we might be a mess, living a life where we are barely scraping along.

When these parts are given permission to come out of the shadows and be heard, understood and allowed to express themselves, they become unburdened. They are happy to be freed of their roles as carriers of our pain, terror and grief. They prefer to be together with us as opposed to separate and forced to carry our most unpleasant memories and sensations. When they integrate with us energetically and emotionally in the present moment, a sense of peace and wholeness develops.

We often work with one part at a time, although one part may activate a cluster of parts that pop up and holler "Pay attention to me too!" They need reassurance that they will have their time to express and integrate but they may have to wait for a while as other parts are attended to first. We are able to identify these unintegrated parts when actions and emotions appear out of the blue. We may recognize that the situation we find ourselves in doesn't warrant the degree of reaction we have to it.

Let me give you an example from my own life. In a past relationship, my partner travelled for work. I would start to pull away a few days before his departure, growing cool and aloof. I would also ignore him for a few days after he returned with an air of, 'Do I know you?' I seemed to be punishing him. I felt a mixture of mad, sad and glad as he was leaving even though I logically knew he was only going away for a brief, work-related trip. These feelings swirled around inside me with no logical explanation. I didn't know what to do with them.

As I became curious about my overly-intense response to his absence, I connected with a younger part of myself that felt sad that he was leaving. Another part of me felt scared of losing him and sad knowing I would miss him. Rather than sharing my feelings and saying "I'm sad that you're leaving, I'm going to miss you," another part of me was angry and wanted to punish him.

When I could connect with these inner parts, I was able to reassure them that he still loved me, that it was safe to share those vulnerable feelings with him. I reminded myself that I could phone him and curl up in his favourite sweater to feel close to him. Once he was out the door, I was no longer triggered at this early attachment level. I could enjoy time to myself, visit with friends, and do more creative work. But when I didn't have an awareness of these activated parts and how to help them, I just felt agitated and distressed—not a great feeling-place for me or my partner.

It's not that these inner impulses, feelings and states go away completely they just get acknowledged sooner and attended to with inner resources that validate, comfort and reassure them. Feelings are energy and flow. They aren't always logical or based in the present. Present situations can trigger past feelings that are unresolved. They often come up from childhood; therefore, they are very young in their thinking and feeling. We don't want those child parts driving the bus. Just as we can't ask our five-year-old self to go out and earn a living for the family, we can't expect these young parts of us to be able to deal with adult situations. They can't—they are too little.

Unacknowledged trauma can be likened to the parable of *The Blind Men and the Elephant*. A group of blind men discover an elephant for the first time and describe it through touching. Because each man is touching a different part of the elephant, their descriptions vary. One feels the ivory tusks, another the tough skin of the elephant's knee, while another the tail, and so on. As they share their findings, they disagree with each other claiming their limited experience is the only "right" one. They failed to 'see' the elephant as described by their collective experiences.

We seem to do much the same thing as we work to heal different parts of the self. Clients often get lost in one part of the self, forgetting in the moment that they are so much more than just that part. If that part of the self has been traumatized and remains unintegrated, it can feel threatened by information from other parts. The felt threat activates a stress response. This part knows that this thing feels like an ivory tusk! That's all there is! It cannot allow for other possibilities because it needs to be ready to defend itself against harm that it has already experienced.

If we can stay calm, however, and reassure the activated, traumatized part that we will take its concerns seriously by being curious about its origins and the current situation, it can calm down and allow other parts to reach out and feel what they are holding, while not losing sight of the current self, or in the case of the blind men, those parts of the elephant that the other men have acknowledged.

As we discussed in Chapter 3—Creativity and Blocks, if we can approach these moments with an open, heart-centred curiosity rather than getting annoyed, irritated or panicked we can see that these parts and the feelings, and experiences they carry, are opportunities for us to heal, become whole and free. We then begin to link the uncomfortable feelings places and the parts that carry them as stepping stones to our happiness and wholeness.

Our creative freedom and emotional awareness grows with each uncomfortable part that is addressed. This allows us to heal, expanding our capacity to be happy and fulfill our goals. It builds self-love. I had a client just this week ask me what the hell is self-love anyway? She has read all about it, is a scholar on the topic but doesn't feel it in her body, physically, energetically, or emotionally. This work is the way to integrate that body piece of the puzzle that holds the answer to that mystery.

Remember the two actors getting ready to go on stage? Both are experiencing butterflies in the stomach, one linking the feelings to excitement, the other linking it to panic and fear. One thinking, *"Oh good. I'm really excited I can feel it. I'm going to have a great show!"* while the other is thinking, *"Oh no! I'm worried. I hate it when I feel that. I'm going to bomb tonight!"*

The same body sensations are in both actors, one embracing the sensations and linking it to a positive experience in the moment of feeling it and therefore anticipating a positive outcome. The other links the same feelings to discomfort, pending doom and disaster. One actor is able to grab the reigns of her/his physical, energetic, emotional body and harness it with confidence and control by leaning into the feelings while the other scrambles away from the feelings, rejecting the moment of the body's experiences, blocking the flow forward. One actor is comfortable with less control, trusting in the moment without fear or need to be seen in a certain way or have a specific outcome. This creates an exhilarating performance both for the actor and audience. You recognize it when you see it.

During IFS therapy, my psychotherapist reminded me that I have a highly developed therapist-self that could hold these younger, scared, split-off parts that hide in the shadows, fearful and guarded. As we worked, I was able to bring a stronger, more mature self to aid these younger parts and help them express what they needed to, freeing them from the past. These young parts were able to integrate with my current Self and be freed of the burdens of the past that they carried for me. I began to feel whole, my energy clearer and my emotions were able to flow more freely.

Even if you are not a therapist, you likely have parts of yourself that you can draw support from as you would if you were with a child who was suffering or scared.

Clients have described a fractured experience of the self in therapy many times. They describe parts of themselves that they wish they didn't have, parts that they even hate and wish they could get rid of once and for all. If they could they would like to carry these parts to the curb and drop them off for the garbage collectors to take away for good. We disown parts of the self, abandon and even abuse them regularly.

But we are 100% recyclable systems. We need all of our energy, emotionality and vitality. As Dr. Richard Schwartz of IFS says "there are no bad parts." Some may be ill-informed but all are trying their hardest to help us. And when they know better they do better.

Trauma often asks that we mature at a rate we aren't able to as we deal with situations beyond our capacities. There is a cost for this to the self. Feelings get shelved, and our young internal parts have to develop faster than they are capable of handling, resulting in anxiety, overwhelm or a feeling of 'never good enough' later in life. Just as feelings aren't always from the present, thoughts and beliefs that we hold aren't always accurate or logical and may have formed when we were younger as well. Even our current body sensations may originate in the past. None of these may apply to our present-day lives, yet they remain alive in us unless we update them to the present.

We need to be able to question and assess the validity of our thoughts, beliefs, feelings and sensations before we act upon them. An over-reaction usually means the presence of a trigger and a part in need of support and attention.

When we become aware enough to share our experiences with people close to us, we build intimacy and connection. Cutting off and shutting down increases suffering for all concerned. Staying open, vulnerable and communicating one's thoughts and feelings deepens connection and strengthens relationships.

First one has to identify what's going on inside, recognize one's defences and feel safe enough to put our guards down. That takes some time and awareness as well as a bank of inner resources.

Are there people or situations that trigger big emotion in you — anger, fear, sorrow? Do you wonder why certain situations or people create such big reactions in you? Does the degree of reaction feel disproportionate to the situation? Then you are likely activating parts of the self that need to be looked into and attended to with curiosity and compassion.

In the process of this work one might have to address guilt, shame, blame, embarrassment, or shyness as well as self-judgement and fear of judgment from others. It's just another layer of our self-protection. Over time as you explore the root causes of these emotions and unburden them, life becomes easier to navigate. You spend less time reacting and more time living in the present. You feel more peace and contentment with life. You attract more experiences that are interesting and pleasurable to you. As you become aware of your thoughts, feelings and sensations, attending to them consciously, you cultivate a feeling of wholeness in your being.

Most of us weren't taught these skills and awareness growing up at home or in school. We're taught to bottle up our emotions. As adults we then project so much onto our partners and react in so many strange and unexplainable ways that it's a wonder any of us can hold ourselves together, let alone build a healthy relationship.

I see couples in counselling where one person is trying to get their partner to provide him or her with what they didn't get emotionally as a child; not surprisingly their partner is confused as to what to do and ultimately fails. They feel like nothing they do is enough. And that's entirely accurate. The partner will never be able to heal that person's wounds from the past. To keep trying to get them to will only cause more suffering and isolation. Our inner parts need us to come to the rescue. Therapeutic support is also helpful both individual and couples work.

Awareness grows as we bring our curiosity to these parts that suffer or react in a triggered fashion to people or situations. If we can remove these intense feelings from others and the situation, and explore their meaning for us, we can offer the parts the support and healing they need. Then we don't need to isolate ourselves or create conflict.

If we can activate our neocortex or thinking brain and bring it online, since it usually goes offline in triggered states, we can talk to the reptilian brain or reactive brain. Our thinking brain has the opportunity to talk the reptilian or instinctual brain down off the ledge—it can be the hero. If the neocortex can be a rational, supportive, calm presence ready to offer support, validation and reassurance to the parts that flare up prepared to fight, flee or freeze, then that part offers great value to the triggered response allowing it to de-escalate, ground and stabilize in the moment.

We can try some inner self-talk between these two parts of the brain. We could begin with a statement from the neocortex like, *"Wow, I see that you feel really upset right now. You seem (angry, scared, sad) I can see and feel that. I'm here for you right now. Let's take some time to be with these feelings; they're important."*

It might be helpful to temporarily remove yourself from this triggering situation if you can't say to the other person that you're feeling triggered right now by something they said or did. If you can do this, you have the opportunity to heal parts of the self and not harm your outer relationships.

This relationship work applies to inner relationships as well as outer ones. I often assist clients to build connections between their inner caregivers and their own disowned, scared, traumatized, isolated parts that don't get the care they need from the caregiver yet witness the caregiver giving to others around her, sometimes all day long.

This is why psychotherapists need to do their own healing as well. We can't always identify our own disowned parts as well as we can those of others. If a friend or client presented these feelings we would know exactly how and what to give for support, but when it comes to ourselves we're at a loss. The links don't seem to be there as obviously as they are in others.

Ultimately wholeness is different from perfection. Wholeness is not about cutting off parts of ourselves we don't like. Wholeness is cultivated through curiosity and non-judgemental acceptance of all our different parts, in whatever stage of healing and integration they're at.

What part of yourself do you wish you could lop off and drop at the curb never to see again? That is the part of the self that most needs your love and attention, acceptance and creativity. For it is is your path to wholeness and freedom. The parts that you least want to look at or acknowledge having are the parts of the self when embraced that will bring you the most return. Creativity can fuel the transformation.

The Blind Men and the Elephant is a story, re-told earlier in this chapter, about parts and how we buy into one part as being the whole reality at times. This part may dominate our experience in the moment and lead us down a rabbit hole of suffering or into a world of fantasy or illusion or deception. Only by holding all the parts simultaneously do we get closer to the whole picture. If we can see a situation from a number of perspectives we can better choose what's best of us. We have more choices that are available.

What is your dominant experience of the self? If there were others tuning into your self what might they find?

In Noh Theatre, The Perfect Flower is an experience one may have once or twice in a lifetime where the individual gazes upon their life as a flower, each petal being one of life's experiences. In that intangible, Perfect Flower moment the beauty of the flower and totality of one's life unites.

Every gesture, movement and play in Noh Theatre is seen as a spiritual quest, embodying the grace and elegance of a flower. The flower is seen as a universal symbol of beauty. Can you see the perfect flower in yourself?

Eckhart Tolle states "We are the universe, the universe is us." There is no separation and the universe seeks to know itself through us and our work is to clear the way for that flow to come through us and be known. With each individual that expression will look absolutely unique but it is, at the same time, one energy or consciousness. Magnificent really. I've always said it doesn't matter where you jump in to the river of creativity, one side or the other, upstream or down it's all the same river so deliberating over whether to paint or sculpt, write or dance is irrelevant since it will all get you there in the end.

When we address our different parts through therapy and with creative exploration through writing, movement, drama, voice and art, an enriched healing process brings these separate parts into visibility and dialogue with the self, resulting in a sense of integrated whole.

This is my belief and my practice both personally and professionally. It is the foundation of self-love and when applied to our partners and communities is also the foundation of healthy loving relationships.

The following exercises offer ways to approach and explore what wholeness means, looks like and feels like for you.

Chapter 11 Exploring Wholeness

Writing

The Good, The Bad and The Ugly Inquiry

1. Write about a part of the self that you wish you could get rid of, take to the curb and have the garbage collectors pick up and remove. See if you can hold an attitude of non-judgemental curiosity and kindness as you examine it through your writing.

Now write about a part of the self that you most like and feel comfortable or proud of. Then write a dialogue between these two parts. Have another person pick up lines from one of these parts and improvise with you in the other part. Then switch. Have two other people play both parts as the author of the work watches. Then write your feelings in each of the roles, how it impacted you. Each role holds valuable information for you.

Blind Feelings

2. Sit blindfolded in a circle as an object, that is a combination of many parts: angled, smooth, small, large, squishy, sandpapery, is passed around. Have each person experience the object through touch gathering their impressions of the object. Remove the object and have everyone take off their blindfolds and write their impressions of the object. Share the results and see how different each person's impressions are.

Partner up with another person and build the object from the combined impressions both in shapes and function. What is its shape - round, flat, twisted? Does it move? What does it do? How does it sound? Allow your imaginations to create a fantasy object that does something practical or non-sensical. Share it with the group.

Sketch a part of the object then move the shapes and colours from your sketch. Create a movement study. Combine these movement with your partner's movements. Incorporate this into your previous movement study.

Visual Art

Perfect Flower Collage

Using collage material, such as magazines, objects from nature, art materials and create an image of your Perfect Flower, an image that captures your whole life in one multi-petalled snapshot. Each petal describes one of life's experiences and the whole image becomes one of a flower of beauty and unity. Choose colours and shapes that best serve your expression. Gather, tear or cut and paste until your flower feels complete. Then gaze upon the whole of it and find its beauty and perfection. Move this image feeling into the unity of the whole self, its innocence and beauty.

Share with others celebrating the diversity and unique creativity of each person's art and movement.

Voice and instrumental accompaniment may be added and a reflection of each person's movements by the group. Celebrate each person's whole self in visual and movement form. Write about your experience and try to hold this feeling of the whole self.

You could take one person's collage and with an explanation by the artist of the parts of their flower, the artist could direct three other people to play the parts of the perfect flower in an improv that the artist watches or may choose to play one of the parts. It can be very powerful to join in or watch as others explore the roles. Then follow it with a write as each part will be experienced by the participant in a unique way. Then share your findings.

Remember there are no mistakes. The Perfect Flower experience of the self is always there if we only knew it. We are all whole right here and now if we only knew it. We have always been whole. There is no separation from the rest of the universe. If we only knew it in every part of the self. This is what I have come to see and experience over many years exploring many parts of the self. Mystery abounds. Not all things an be explained so simply. It's a big universe out there.

Chapter 12

Creativity and Altered States

C reative exploration of a certain kind can take you into 'altered' states. Then there are further states explored by some that break through the ceiling of this reality to other places and times where mystery abounds.

Many people go through their lives without experiencing altered states naturally. Some take substances to experience these states of consciousness but some people go there without the addition of anything. Unexplainable events have happened throughout my life. I have memories of them from childhood, possibly brought on originally through physical, emotional trauma or a vivid imagination, a combination of both or an explanation beyond either of these possibilities. Some people are terrified of altered states they hear of or touch into. This is understandable. Encouraging these experiences isn't right for everyone. I didn't actively seek them out. They found me.

I'm not sure it's something one can actively nurture within oneself. I do have some exercises that I recommend before and after creative work that builds the container for creative travel into the unknown. 'Only go as far as you know how to get back' is a statement I've used in teaching over the years, yet some people need help identifying what that boundary is for them. I've learned to consciously hold one's creative space so that safety is maintained for myself and for others.

Marking entry and exit from the work is important to make sure you ground yourself in a day-to-day mind state when you leave your creative space. I sometimes set an alarm to mark the time passing when I'm working creatively just so I remember to pause, drink, pee, eat and stretch. Hunkering in and hunkering out is a term I learned in physical theatre that marks the beginning and of creative work and will be described in detail in the exercises section at the end of this chapter. This practice allows one to enter into the creative work and exit it at the end of the day, returning to the everyday self.

Linda Putnam, one of my physical theatre teachers, called this self that's living in a day-to-day reality 'the breakfast table person.' If we say we are going to pick up milk on the way home from class we need to remember to do that. We pick up the self that made that promise — the person we were at the breakfast table that morning.

In creative work we leave this every day self behind us; we become other characters, explore non-human forms and raw, unpolished, exaggerated emotions. We are not expected to behave in creative work the way we would in public or in a social setting with friends. We explore the absurd, the obnoxious, the rude, the abandoned and abandoning, the shadow and the transcendent self. We shed social norms and explore impulse — even the banned behaviours that we know to be 'wrong.' There needs to be an established rule of safety and an understanding that nothing will be taken personally before we are able to explore all our possible impulses without harming ourselves or others.

I have experienced a third level of reality, one beyond the everyday self and the creative self, a level of reality that travelled alongside or outside the reality of my everyday self — the 'fetch wood, carry water' self and greater than the experiences in my creative life. Then, unexplainable events would occur. I would dip into an expanded reality for a period of time and then just as effortlessly return to the creative self or the everyday self. I would often ignore what just happened since I had no way to make sense of it or hold onto it.

It's said that European explorers approaching the New World in ships were not visible to the natives as they had no preconception of a ship or mental framework for one, so they couldn't actually see them.

There are a number of theories. Some say that the ships were so alien to the natives experience that they might have seen them but pretended not to, believing they were spirits, possibly harmful in nature and if ignored might just keep moving along and not bother them. It was said that the shamans of the native tribes were the first to see and acknowledge their existence.

So how does this relate to my strange events? We have a saying in theatre, "I'll do it but I won't watch," meaning one part of me shows up for the moment while other parts simultaneously disappear or refuse to acknowledge that I have just said or done what I have. In my personal experience, when these unusual, extraordinary events occurred, I would experience them, then immediately move on as if they hadn't just happened, while knowing they had on another level. I compartmentalized them and stored them in a place inside that was separate from my everyday self.

I would never have dreamed of gathering up all of these events, writing them down and sharing them with others. What will others think? It's unsettling just thinking about it as I write this. I have a reputation to uphold. But these events have stayed with me over many years. They are as clear today as when they happened and that seems to make them worth exploring and sharing now.

Joseph Campbell says, "The cave you fear to enter holds the treasure you seek." I suppose I perceive these events as possibly holding some secrets that I would like to explore further. Many of these events took place in highly creative moments.

Jerome Frank, former Professor of Psychiatry at John Hopkins, considered to be one of the most influential theorists about psychotherapy, considers the possible role of psychic abilities in psychotherapy. *In Cognition and Psychotherapy, 2nd ed.* 2004, he writes:

"Our own hunch, which I mention with some trepidation, is that the most gifted therapists may have telepathic, clairvoyant, or other parapsychological abilities. They may, in addition, possess something ... that can only be termed 'healing power.'"

What has my role as an artist, teacher and therapist played in having these otherworldly experiences? Does a life led by creativity and curiosity lend itself to more of these experiences? Does a life that has experienced trauma and injury open a doorway to psychic sensibilities that would otherwise be closed? These questions are fuelling a curiosity for what's hidden beneath the surface.

These are my personal experiences of life's mystery. I am on a unique search for answers to puzzling questions concerning the mysteries of life, higher purpose, and the workings of the universe.

If I were embarking on a hike, I would now have my backpack, a map, a canteen of water and a snack ready to follow the trail and engage with nature. This inner adventure is not so straight forward or so easily explained. A different supply of inner resources is packed and ready for departure on this mysterious journey inward, ready to meet what's new, unformed or un-birthed as of yet. The following is one such experience of mystery and power for me

Women's Penitentiary, Kingston

I worked during the summer of '86 with Theatre Ontario at Queen's University in Kingston, teaching creative movement to students enrolled in a variety of classes related to acting. I taught them physical theatre, movement and voice. Many of them were elementary and high school teachers on summer vacation, adding professional development credits while learning playful, creative skills to take back to the classroom.

I taught two-hour classes, back to back, running the entire day, except for a lunch break. Classes were heavily concentrated, challenging and creative. Each day required an enormous output of energy and creativity. It was one of the most intense weeks of teaching I have ever done.

On one occasion I was taking my welcome, much needed, mid-day break, with a brown bag lunch in hand, heading down to sit near the water for some fresh air, sunshine and a change of scenery to refuel for the afternoon teaching sessions.

My path to the water passed a large, sturdy white stone building, its title carved boldly out of stone above heavily enforced double front doors, Prison for Women. Just as I passed the sidewalk leading up to the front doors I heard a prolonged high-pitched, blood-curdling scream discharge from an upper window. It was the sound of pure pain and anguish, the cry of a terrified, desperate, severely wounded soul causing a visceral reaction in my nervous system, emotions and physical body.

I had studied the work of Alfred Wolfsohn who wrote about this cry on the battlefields of WW I where he served as a medic removing the wounded and dying soldiers.

I was stopped in my tracks, now facing the prison walkway and front doors, the sound resonating through my cells. Time and space fell away. In that moment, I had a mystical experience I will never forget. I had a profound sense that the woman inside the prison and I were one. There was no separation between us, just one body, one being.

A question arose from somewhere deep within and I asked, "If we are the same (and I felt that to be true) then why is she in there doing that and I'm out here, doing this?"

The answer came in the form of a lightning bolt of energy down from above, entering through the top of my head, travelling through the centre of my body and exiting out through my feet into the earth. Along with the lightning bold which was not unpleasant in any way, there was a waterfall effect of energy flowing down through my body.

Following this experience, without knowing exactly why, I then replied, "Oh, I see," satisfied that my question had been fully answered. I understood something at a level beneath logical reasoning and intellect. The whole experience may have taken only a few minutes, and yet it felt timeless. I continued my walk to the water, ate lunch and returned to class. Today, thirty-five years later, I remember it as if it were yesterday. It remains very alive in my body.

Alfred Wolfsohn (September 23, 1896 – February 5, 1962) was a German singing teacher who suffered from recurring auditory hallucinations of screaming soldiers, whom he had witnessed dying from wounds in World War I as a stretcher-bearer. After the war he was diagnosed with Shell Shock, a form of trauma. Wolfsohn did not respond to hospitalization or psychiatric treatment, but later cured himself by 'vocalizing extreme sounds', bringing about what he called a catharsis and exorcism.

Out of this practice he developed vocal techniques and exercises using the full range and expressiveness of his voice. Wolfsohn began teaching others, acting as both a singing teacher and psychotherapist, seeking to combine the principle of both disciplines. Wolfsohn had no formal training in voice work or psychotherapy but nonetheless became a critic of traditional vocal pedagogy and an advocate for the principles of Analytical Psychology developed by Carl Jung.

The aim of his lessons was to help students extend the range and expressiveness of their voice to include every possible vocal sound, which he believed both represented and precipitated the realization of increased human potential in other areas of life. He wondered how he could help performers to develop the depth of vocal/physical connection he had experienced in the dying soldiers when the actors were not in crisis situations. It became the basis of his work.

He pioneered voice research not only as an instrument of artistic expression but also of human development, psychology and therapy. Wolfsohn stated, "The voice is the muscle of the soul." Wolfsohn's philosophy was that one had to go into the depths to fight the furies and demons, into the depths of oneself, before one can rise to the heights of understanding and creativity. In the same way, one has to find the depths in one's own voice before one can be able to reach heights, not merely in range but in the depths and heights of expression – and it is on this that his teaching was based.

He subscribed to the views of Carl Jung, who proposed that each human psyche comprises a composite of subpersonalities that appear most vividly in dreams. Wolfsohn sought to enable the expression of these subpersonalities through distinct vocal sounds.

When Wolfsohn died in 1962 a group of his students continued to train in voice work with Roy Hart, a South African actor and long time student of Wolfsohn. The group became The Roy Hart Theatre and in 1974 they moved to the South of France to establish a permanent rehearsal studio, school, and drama troupe. Roy Hart died in a car accident a year later, but the remaining members continued to produce experimental theatre and music productions and teach the approach to vocal expression initially established by Wolfsohn.

Why all this inquiry into Wolfsohn? Because it links dramatically to the moment I experienced outside of the prison in Kingston on that sunny day and experienced the cry from inside. It was unlikely that woman was on her deathbed, but she was expressing the pain, defeat and utter anguish of her life. The intensity of it was apparent in her one, gut-wrenching outcry. The sound that she produced released an explosion of energy, expansion and dissolution in me. I merged with her through her cry and was transported to an experience of universal love and oneness.

I believe this is what Wolfsohn spoke of with the cries of soldiers in battle. One major difference between his experience and my own was that his experience was repeated and prolonged, developing trauma and PTSD for him. Hearing one of those gut-wrenching cries I was catapulted into a profound experience of spiritual transcendence. I related to Wolfsohn's description of the power of the human voice to carry emotion and communicate at a soul level. I had a first hand experience of how sound can become a bridge to other levels of reality, creativity, healing and relationship.

It's important to state here that I do not practice or promote this level of exploration in my psychotherapy practice or my creative life today. It's a part of my past, before entering into the healing profession.

Altered States – Hunkering In and Out

Following classes where I was teaching physical theatre and movement I would find myself in altered states of space and time. Creative work can cause that.

One of my most influential physical theatre teachers, Linda Putnam, taught us to "hunker in" and "hunker out" of the work. We were to leave our 'breakfast table person' outside the studio as we entered the work. The work did not have the same rules and boundaries as the outside world. For example, an actor may explore rude sounds, gesture and words as part of building their character for a scene.

There were firm safety rules within the work. No harm could be done to self, others or the surroundings. Beyond that, the envelope stretched as far as one chose to take it. "Only go as far as you know how to get back," was a statement Linda Putnam used with us and I later adopted as a teacher. But I found that not everyone knew when to turn back and I was there to intervene in those rare cases as holder of the space.

In order to 'hunker in' and 'hunker out' we would strike a balance position. One may be crouched in a balance on one's heels, bent knees or a modified stance, depending on the person's flexibility. It had to be a balance position that you worked at to sustain, with some degree of concentration. Then a contract was made for the day's work, its length of time, goals and intentions. We would then fall forwards out of the balance position into the work. At the end of the day we would return to the same balance position, reflect on the day's work and complete the contract. We would then fall back, out of the balance position. This marked a clear difference of outside life to inside work and the reverse.

I recall leaving a movement class with the Grad theatre students at York University in one of those altered states. At that time, I was not always aware when I was in them. On this particular day, I stood beside my car in the parking lot, holding my keys, thinking "Now I know these go somewhere, but I'm not sure where." The everyday world requires a different awareness than that needed in creative work.

Needless to say, I hadn't 'hunkered out' that day at York University and it certainly showed. Luckily, I made it to my destination safely, by car.

A Conversation in Time

I was working with the Crows Theatre, in Toronto. They had hired me to help with character development. They had built masks and I was interviewing them, individually, to build back-stories, physical characteristics and movement. I interviewed each actor in mask in front of the company as audience.

One actor came out and sat on a chair in front us. I began my usual interview questions much like you would see on a television talk show. Then something very strange happened. I slipped into another time period. For the rest of the interview I was speaking Olde English. The cast was mesmerized. They sat observing the exchange I was having with this actor. They probably assumed I had studied the language of that time period as had the actor. Yet neither of us had. I knew nothing of the language of that period let alone have the ability to speak it fluently. It would be similar to speaking Shakespearean text naturally as your mother tongue.

It was a surreal, altered space and time. The only thing that I remembered when it was over was the last line I spoke, "Well be gone with you then." I had travelled to another time period and met an old friend wearing the mask and had a conversation.

Was it a past life for him and me? I don't know. I felt I had known him and had had a satisfying visit, just like old times. The curtain was lifted for a brief moment to challenge once again, my sense of reality.

A Visit on the Astral Plane

Another experience I had with psychic overtones was with an actor at York University in the Grad Theatre Dept. The students were performing *A Streetcar Named Desire*. It was the day before opening. We had worked very hard on it for a couple of weeks. Susan was playing the role of *Blanche Dubois*. We were putting finishing touches to her character that day in class.

That night I awoke with a start, bolting upright. Crouched beside my bed, staring into my face, only inches away, was a ghostly figure that I immediately recognized as Susan. I said, "Oh Susan, you scared me!" She just continued to stare at me with an intense, pensive stare. I intuitively responded, "Yes, I'll be there tomorrow. Everything will go well." I reassured her that she was ready and would make a great Blanche Dubois. I told her I'd see her soon and rolled over and went back to sleep.

First thing in the morning my phone rang and it was Susan. She said she didn't know why she was calling me. I laughed and told her that I think I knew why. She had paid me a visit, on the *astral plane*, in the middle of the night checking to be sure I was there. I told her that she had scared me half to death before I recognized that it was her. She was puzzled by the whole event but we both had a chuckle.

We met at the company's warm up later that day and she did, in fact, perform a brilliant Blanche Dubois. We've remained good friends ever since.

Other Creative Experiences

I have had experiences in the studio painting where I 'slipped the screen' or slid into an altered reality, losing track of time and space. I once said, "I'm just going to finish the corner of my sculpture and then I'm off to bed."

210

Seemingly moments later, I looked up and it was 7 am, ten hours later. Time had vanished, sleepiness with it. My experience of the creative self is that she drops all of the usual needs when she enters the creative zone. There is a sense of interconnectedness to everything or a sense of one-ness married with a sense of 'there are no mistakes, it isn't possible to make one' is intoxicating.

I have experienced this altered and time and space quality many times in *Authentic Movement* as well as in art. We are moving when we are painting. It is a fearless space where there are no mistakes only curiosity, discover and flow. Any impulse is welcome and may appear– scraping, blotting, washing, pouring, sanding, chopping, whatever arrives at the door. Physically engaging with the art materials in an impulse-by-impulse way with no preconceived notion of outcome creates a certain freshness in the work. Be grateful for whatever comes.

Cy Twombly states;

"We think we can lay hold of the image and take it captive, but the docile captive is not the real image, but only the idea, which is the image with its character beaten out of it ... The image is the raw material of idea. It cannot be dispossessed of the primordial freshness, which ideas can never claim. An idea is a derivative and tamed, the image is in the natural or wild state and has to be discovered there, not put there, obeying it's own law and none of ours."

Once you have a goal in mind, the creative process becomes limited and you lose the raw, creative potential within the process and the outcome suffers.

"All suffering is bearable if it is seen as part of a story."

~ Isak Dinesen

I hope by honouring these stories and memories I will discover their deeper mystery and they will creatively lead me to more understanding of life and creativity. My growing experience is one where the world isn't nearly as neat and tidy as we'd like to think it is. It's vastly unexplainable and mysterious. Magic abounds and a creative life invites one into that if you're receptive and dare to go. As I stated earlier it's good to have resources with you, including some therapy under your belt as the path can be furious and frightful.

Has my life as an artist, teacher and therapist invited these otherworldly experiences or have otherworldly aspects of me, always having been there, attracted and shaped the path of my life? Does a life led by creativity and curiosity lend itself to having more of these experiences or does an expansive soul look for outlets to express through resulting in unexplainable events? Does a life that has experienced trauma and injury have greater access to psychic experiences than a soul that hasn't or does a soul that's open to exploring the depths of life's experience, even those embedded in the trauma, seek its deeper meaning even when the going gets tough?

"Why Me?" I ask. "Just because ... why not?" is the response (Spirit's sense of humour). "What is the higher purpose of these events? Am I getting the full evolutionary benefit?" I ask. "Of course not!" is the answer, again accompanied by a chuckle. I seem to be entertaining the Higher Self with my barrage of questions. But there is such an infinite, large-hearted love surrounding the voice answering my finite and finicky questions that I feel at peace.

Having gathered these extraordinary events into one basket, I see them as a rich resource for my creative life. Moving to a place where one can hold them along with the possibility of some reality or realities so beyond the day-to-day is exciting, invigorating and oh, so creatively exciting.

Chapter 12 Exploring Altered States

Multi-Modal Exercise for Altered States

Have you had any altered state experiences in your lifetime that you could write down, gather images for or create movements for? If not then allow yourself to enter into your imagination and play with what it might look like, if you could. Search for a character out of time and interact with her or him. What extraordinary abilities might you possess? See where it leads.

Conclusion

As we come to the end of this journey of healing through creativity, I'm hoping you take with you these important ideas.

We are 100% renewable – organically designed to be whole. It takes enormous energy to live in an un-integrated state. If you feel exhausted, tense or blocked you are likely holding some of your energy and emotion in parts of the self that are cut-off, separate and suppressed. There is often shame, guilt or judgement towards these parts of the self, from within the self. They subsequently get projected onto others around you as a way to be seen and resolved.

If you recognize that you are doing this, I hope you can hold these parts with compassion rather than judging them. We all do this as a brilliant survival mechanism so we can cope with life until we can repair, retrieve and heal ourselves.

Creativity and emotional support have the ability to take us on a search for these lost parts of the self, find them, embrace them and allow them to express and release the stories and feelings they have been carrying for us. Consciously or not, we are either blocking and resisting the natural flow towards connection, integration and wholeness, or we are unfolding , healing and moving towards it.

This book has collected my experiences, bringing together separate parts of the self that held stories and experiences from the past. I was able to finally see them and see myself as one unified whole—a major accomplishment for a fractured soul.

The *Perfect Flower* in Noh Theatre describes this experience beautifully. Each petal is seen as one of life's experiences. In the Perfect Flower moment one is able to see and take in the whole of life's experiences as one does with the beauty of a flower, its presence and natural perfection.

It is my hope that you, the reader may capture a glimpse of your own Perfect Flower—your life as a whole—perfect in its own way, beautifully flawed and full of grace. I hope that through this writing and these exercises in a variety of modalities you have found ways to open the creative flow and mystery that lives in you.

Understanding how and why you block your creativity and discovering ways to approach the barriers so that you can find the door and be invited inside, is a critical piece to the whole puzzle. Finding your own unique voice through a variety of approaches—movement, art, writing—will appeal to different parts of the self, some more comfortably than others.

I hope that you have found and continue to find the support needed for the challenges that promote your growth and expansion creatively and consciously. It doesn't matter where you jump into the river of creativity and life, upstream or down, right bank or left, it's all the same river leading us home to the self .

216

But there is much fear that arises along the way and we need emotional support with that so we don't back down, buying the warnings at face value. They want us to stop and withdraw into what feels like a safe spot. The spot that feels safe may also be the place where you won't grow into your full, potential, vibrant self. I want that vibrancy for each one of you.

Blocks can be as exciting, creatively, as the moments when we are creatively flowing. In fact they may be even more exciting as they indicate that we are on the precipice of something very new for us. All creation is new and therefore unfamiliar and usually scary for us to venture into. How do we hold the frightened parts that are saying "No, don't go there!" when we are on the edge of a breakthrough moment? Holding blocks with the gentleness, respect and curiosity they deserve while reassuring ourselves that we are safe and secure will support the scary journey into the deeper layers of the self. It's an infinite journey with great reward to our sense of freedom and joy.

Every drop of tension in the physical body holds infinite creative impulses. It's the way our bodies speak to us. The body is saying, "I'm an open book you just don't know how to read." This book hopefully has helped you read the body and your emotions so that you feel equipped to live the creative, and vibrant life you were meant to live in the full brilliance that is you.

You have the tools now to fly like the bird off of the back of the Wildebeest, free and unencumbered while embracing and loving every aspect of the Wildebeest that you encounter along the way on your unique journey to wholeness.

Endnotes

My Master's thesis was, in part, based on Rudolf Laban's Eight Effort Actions embracing weight, space, time and flow. In it's simplest form, since it can get quite sophisticated;

- Weight is heavy/light
- Space is direct/indirect
- Time is fast/slow
- Flow is free/bound

When we combine weight, space and time in their various combinations, we get 8 basic movement results;

1. <u>Slash</u>   *heavy weight, indirect space and fast time*
2. <u>Punch</u>   *heavy, direct and fast*
3. <u>Wring</u>   *heavy, indirect and slow*
4. <u>Press</u>   *heavy, direct and slow*
5. <u>Flick</u>   *light, indirect and fast*
6. <u>Dab</u>   *light, direct and fast*
7. <u>Float</u>   *light, indirect and slow*
8. <u>Glide</u>   *light, indirect and slow*

Flow - free or bound, may apply to any of the effort actions, although the heavy weight actions tend to have a more bound flow than the light actions which tend to be freer in flow. Looked at another way;

	Weight		Space		Time		Flow	
	Heavy	Light	Direct	Indirect	Fast	Slow	Free	Bound
Slash	✓			✓	✓		✓	✓
Punch	✓		✓		✓		✓	✓
Wring	✓			✓		✓	✓	✓
Press	✓		✓			✓	✓	✓
Flick		✓		✓	✓		✓	✓
Dab		✓	✓		✓		✓	✓
Float		✓		✓		✓	✓	✓
Glide		✓		✓		✓	✓	✓

The table above shows the eight effort actions in the first column followed by their associated characteristics in the following columns. The black and grey check marks in the Flow columns indicate the primary mode of flow in black with the secondary mode in grey.

Catherine Marrion on Gibberish

A friend and colleague, Catherine Marrion, art therapist and actor who studied with Keith Johnstone, founder of International TheatreSports Institute, wrote this about gibberish.

"Left to their own devices many newbies do gibberish that sounds very inarticulate and unspecific, much like a sloppy drunk — vowels sliding around without much to hold them in. His method was to ask us to write sentences of gibberish on a piece of paper. Make some sentences long and some short, and the end punctuation can be a period, a question mark or an exclamation point. Then he paired people off and had us do scenes using our gibberish scripts — we could take turns (one sentence each), or just see how

much or how little we want to say in response to our partner. We circulated around, doing our scripts with different people, and by the time we had finished, we were already becoming quite fluent in our own personal gibberish and beginning to improvise more text in our own invented dialect. This method gives newbies 'training wheels,' and takes the pressure off inventing and gives some time to get into the fun of it. Then the training wheels come off and away we go!"

Thanks Catherine.

Recommended Resources

Richard C Schwartz Ph.D.
You are the One You've Been Waiting For
    Center for Self Leadership (2008)
        ISBN 978-0615249322

Internal Family Systems Therapy
    The Guilford Press; Second edition (2019)
        ISBN 978-1462541461

Bessel Van Der Kolk MD.
The Body Keeps the Score: Brain, Mind, and Body in the Healing of Trauma
    Penguin Books (2015)
        ISBN 978-0143127741

Peter A Levine Ph.D.

Waking the Tiger; Healing Trauma
North Atlantic Books (1997)
ISBN 978-1556432330

In an Unspoken Voice; How the Body Releases Trauma and Restores Goodness
North Atlantic Books (2010)
ISBN 978-1556439438

Pat Ogden Ph.D.

Trauma and the Body: A Neurobiologically Informed Approach To Clinical Practice
WW Norton (Sept. 19 2006)
ISBN 978-0393704570

John H. Lee

Facing the Fire; Experiencing and Expressing Anger Appropriately
Bantam (June 1 1993)
ISBN 978-0553372403

The Anger Solution; The Proven Method for Achieving Calm and Developing Healthy, Long-Lasting Relationships
Da Capo Lifelong Books (Aug. 11 2009)
ISBN 978-0738212609

John Bradshaw

Healing the Shame the Binds You
Health Communications Inc; Recovery Classics Edition
ISBN-13: 978-0757303234

Gabor Maté MD.

When the Body Says No; The Cost of Hidden Stress
Vintage Canada; 1 edition (Feb. 3 2004)
ISBN 978-0676973129

Brené Brown Ph.D., LMSW

Daring Greatly: How the Courage to Be Vulnerable Transforms the Way We Live, Love, Parent, and Lead
Avery; Reprint edition (April 7 2015)
ISBN 978-1592408412

Gifts of Imperfection; Let Go of Who You Think You're Supposed to Be and Embrace Who You Are
Hazelden Publishing; 1st Edition edition (2010)
ISBN 978-1592858491

Michael A. Singer

The Untethered Soul; The Journey Beyond Yourself
New Harbinger Publications; 1 edition (2007)
ISBN 978-1572245372

Emilie Conrad

Life on Land; The Story of Continuum
North Atlantic Books; 1 edition (2007)
ISBN 978-1556436451

Elinor Dickson Ph.D

Dancing at the Still Point; Marion Woodman, SOPHIA, and Me
Chiron Publications (2019)
ISBN 978-1630516956

A.H. Almaas

Diamond Heart; Elements of the Real in Man
    Shambhala (2000)
        ISBN 978-0834823846

Paula Thomson PsyD

Creativity, Trauma, and Resilience
    Lexington Books (2020)
        ISBN 978-1498560221

Dawna Markova Ph.D

No Enemies Within; A Creative Process for Discovering What's Right About What's Wrong
    Red Wheel/Weiser (1994)
        ISBN 978-0943233642

Techniques For Stress Reduction on YouTube

Donna Eden,
    Energy Medicine

Nick Ortner,
    Emotional Freedom Technique (EFT Tapping)

Byron Katie,
    The Work

Related Short Stories

Material Witness

Material Witness is a creative non-fiction story that I read in Muskoka at a summer book launch of Wildebeest, 2020. It's about creativity, impulse and inner parts in conversation.

It isn't easy being fully present. Well, it's really easy once you're there, it's getting there that's the hard part. I know I'm in 'the zone' when I no longer feel anxious about making mistakes. There are no mistakes 'in the zone' … only curiosity, discovery and flow.

But even then, I wonder which impulses are really mine and which ones are learned behaviours, coping mechanisms from past experiences with family, friends, lovers and others.

I was introduced to creativity growing up with an artist as mother. Her craft was sewing which she would do day in and day out if left to her own devices. Some kids had a tooth fairy. I had a clothing fairy. It wasn't unusual to wake up to a new outfit magically draped over the end of my bed, a pink polka dot top and shorts with a matching miniature outfit for barbie, sewn from the scraps.

It never occurred to me that my mother had a compulsive sewing disorder,

with sleepless nights and rapid, hormonal, mood swings. I thought she was 'normal.'

During the day her art-making was laced with frustration. A steady stream of profanity poured from chapped lips as coarse hands forced the fabric through the sewing machine's runaway, hammering needle … full speed, pedal to the metal. When it couldn't take any more pressure, the needle would snap off, mid seam and a stream of pent-up rage flew through the air like cows in a tornado. "Shit, damn it, oh hell."

In time, a second creative emerged in the family, me. An artist with multiple voices and modes of expression in writing, movement and visual art. Now, my painter self stands in front of the canvas, waiting, "I need to mess up the white, pristine canvas so its blank emptiness no longer terrifies me." I get an impulse to use black. "What! Black! No! You can't use black!" There's nowhere to go from there! It's limiting! The louder the protest from head office the deeper the impulse digs in and persists.

Inside the creativity pinball machine, I bounce off the pegs, one after another. The ball remains in play in spite of the critic's tirade, "Don't touch it. You'll wreck it. Pick something smaller. You're wasting paint!"

I confront my attacker, "It's only canvas and paint. I have more of both. It's okay if I wreck it. I don't care. This is for me. Remember, it's all about process vs product. I'm free to explore, be outrageous, line the garbage can with it if I want. You're not in control here! So back off!"

I take my canvas to the basin and soak it thoroughly with water, lay it flat and begin to pour black India ink over its surface. My body releases a long-held breath and my belly relaxes. I feel the tug of some primal longing that I can't describe.

The ink hits the water and magic begins. I tilt, pour, blow and blot the surface, adding a second colour, Paynes Grey. It's still very dark, a blue-grey with purple overtones. The voice of the critic returns but with less weight, fading as I move towards a lighter, quieter place of expanded possibility. I mix white with grey, blue and black creating a range of new colours, warm to cool, light to dark, subtle to strong.

The unnamed, indescribable longing is now met.

Shapes begin to appear in the form of milkweeds. They speak to me these days. I'm moved by the beauty of a mature milkweed, long after the Monarchs have pollinated and the larvae have fed, when the mature pods burst into feathery seeds that float through the air on tufts of white silk.

A dried milkweed sits on my desk in the office and a painting of one hangs on the wall. They remind me of the beauty and sensuality of nature, our nature, my true nature. The one that embodies presence. The presence I return to and rediscover each time I drop into flow.

Wild State

Wild State tells the story of inner parts at play in the art studio when no one is watching, and creative body impulses are free to lead the way.

As a clown, I performed a strip tease to "You Can Leave Your Hat On" by Etta James at a painting retreat in the Hockley Valley taught by Pat Fairhead, a watercolour artist and friend.

Pat was the best audience a clown could ever have. Her eyes would bulge to twice their size, eyebrows fly up to her hairline, swallowing her forehead while her jaw dropped open in a mixture of shock, disbelief and delight, cradled in child's unbridled innocence. She would gasp for air on the inhale and roar with laughter on the out.

The more outrageous I got, the louder she roared, the louder she roared, the freer I felt and the more outrageous I became. We played off of each other.

But there's a back-story to all of this. Earlier in the day, I led the artists through a gentle warm on the deck of the cottage in the morning sun - stretching, curling, twisting, breathing in and breathing out, swinging limbs to loosen tight muscles in preparation for the painters task of capturing subtle nuances of light and land.

I stayed behind with a different set of needs.

I had the whole place to myself…a row of tables in a large sun-lit studio where I could stretch out – laying out 6 large sheets of watercolour paper; one hundred and forty pound, acid free, hot press Fabriano, 100% cotton, extra white, coarse finish with no distractions.

I was drawing, splattering, scraping, sanding, dabbing, blotting, flicking and splashing in a cascade of impulse to image. Cy Twombly says an image must be discovered in its natural or wild state obeying its own laws and none of ours, otherwise we end up with an idea, which is an image with its character beaten out of it, tamed and robbed of its primordial freshness.

A thought surfaces, "My clothes are too tight! They're too confining! They're inhibiting my flow.

Another responds immediately, "Well, there's no one here... You have the whole place to yourself. Why not? What harm could it do?"

Off comes my blouse and shorts with effortless speed and I continue to paint from a newfound physical freedom-....(pause) then another impulse arrives. It's stronger having picked up momentum and intensity from the last, "My bra and panties are strangling me! I hate them. They've gotta go. Now!

Seconds later they're parachuting through the air with reckless abandon.

Ah, free at last.

The summer breeze caresses my naked body moving gently over its smooth surfaces and into its tiny creases. Impulses ebb and flow as paintings materialize one after another, after another. It's an effortless place where there are no mistakes and time melts away.

I see my white, cotton blouse billowing softly in the breeze. It becomes a blank canvas begging to be adorned with all the gusto of a Klimt Kiss. I splash, splatter, sponge, squeeze and squish it with an animal passion and persistence…my bare body becomes Klimt.

Then another impulse bubbles up from the cauldron belly below. It's a physical urge to hang upside down. I clear one of the tables with a wet forearm, climb up onto it and hang over the edge, bum in the air, head and upper body dangling towards the floor, toes curled over the opposite edge to counterbalance my weight while adding the finishing touches to my blouse art.

By this time paintings cover every available surface of the studio in a wild array of shapes, colours and textures. My body is an abstract in a room of abstraction. (pause)

From what seems like a thousand miles away and in a place where time has no baring I hear a 'click, click' of the outside door and a soft murmur of voices in light conversation.

(GASP) OMG The painters are back. I'm catapulted back in time like a time traveller of the universe landing on the head of a pin.

I launch into action in a frantic scramble to find cover. My underwear is nowhere to be found. I grab my painted blouse and pull it on in a frenzy. "Buttons, button holes how the hell do they work?" I can't remember. My thinking brain is off line, left behind, still wet but so am I.

I'm a bit shaken and shaking a bit when the painters round the corner of the studio door. They stop dead in their tracks looking shocked, some offended, some, I think, even disgusted by what they see. I don't know what to do or what to say, where to go or what to feel.

230

Then Pat rounds the corner, gasps with shock and delight and roars with laughter and I exhale. After a moment of stunned confusion the others follow suite with cautious, somewhat awkward chuckles.

Pat wanders through the room observing the work, "Oh, I like that and THAT, wow, that's good." I exhale again with more ease as she weaves her way over to where I'm standing, leans in and whispers in my ear,

F*ck 'em if they can't take the heat.

Art

The art pieces on the following pages were chosen as they relate to the theme of creativity as a way to awaken and assist one in the healing process. They led me to parts of my self that were unknown to me. When they appeared, seemingly out-of-the-blue, through the process of art-making, were undeniable.

For example, building the mask, *Animal Urges*, revealed deep-seated fear. I have performed many monologues and songs in this mask. One song by Liz Noton, titled, *"I'm Too Rough For You Honey."* The art pieces, titled *She Speaks* and *Body Matters* explore healing from sexual abuse.

Each image speaks its personal story to me. Since visual art has always been an important mode of expression and healing for me, I felt it needed to be represented here.

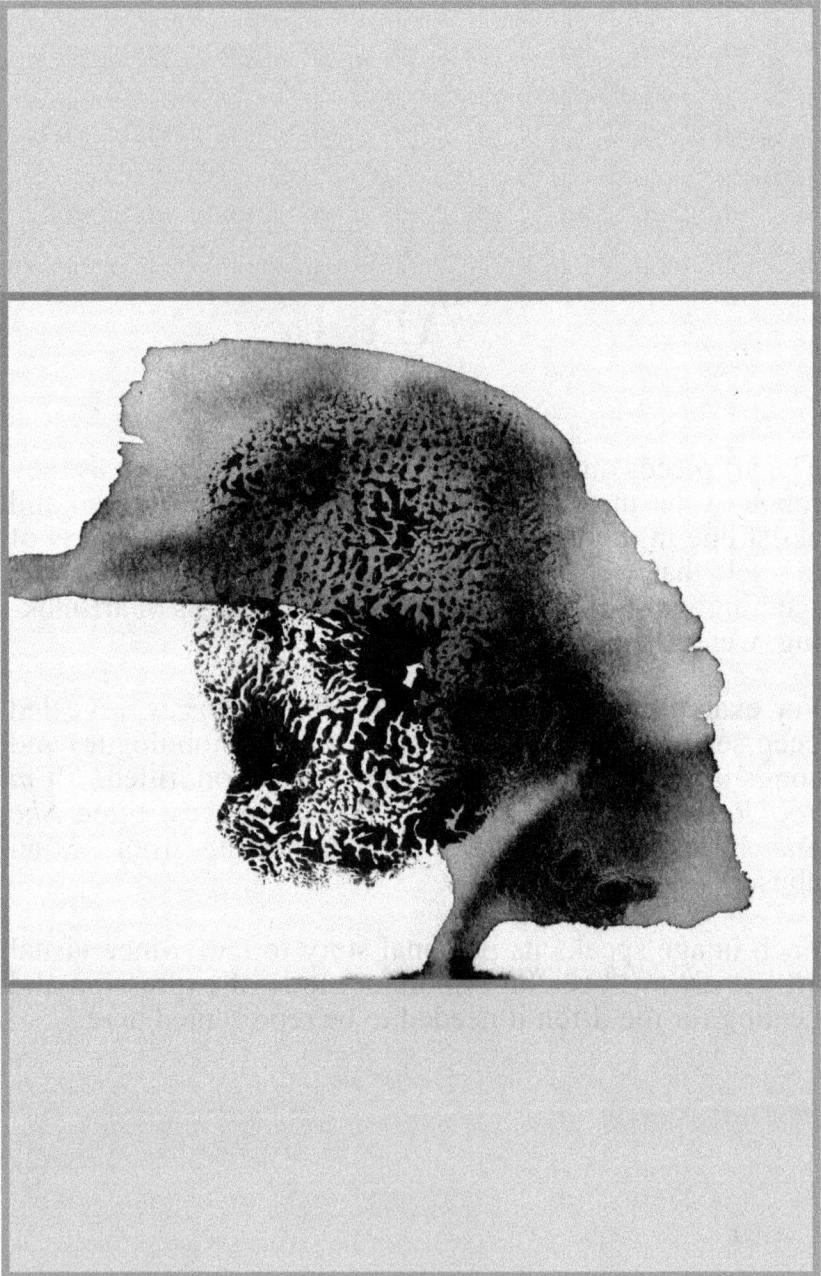

New Ideas
8"x10"
Ink and acrylic on paper

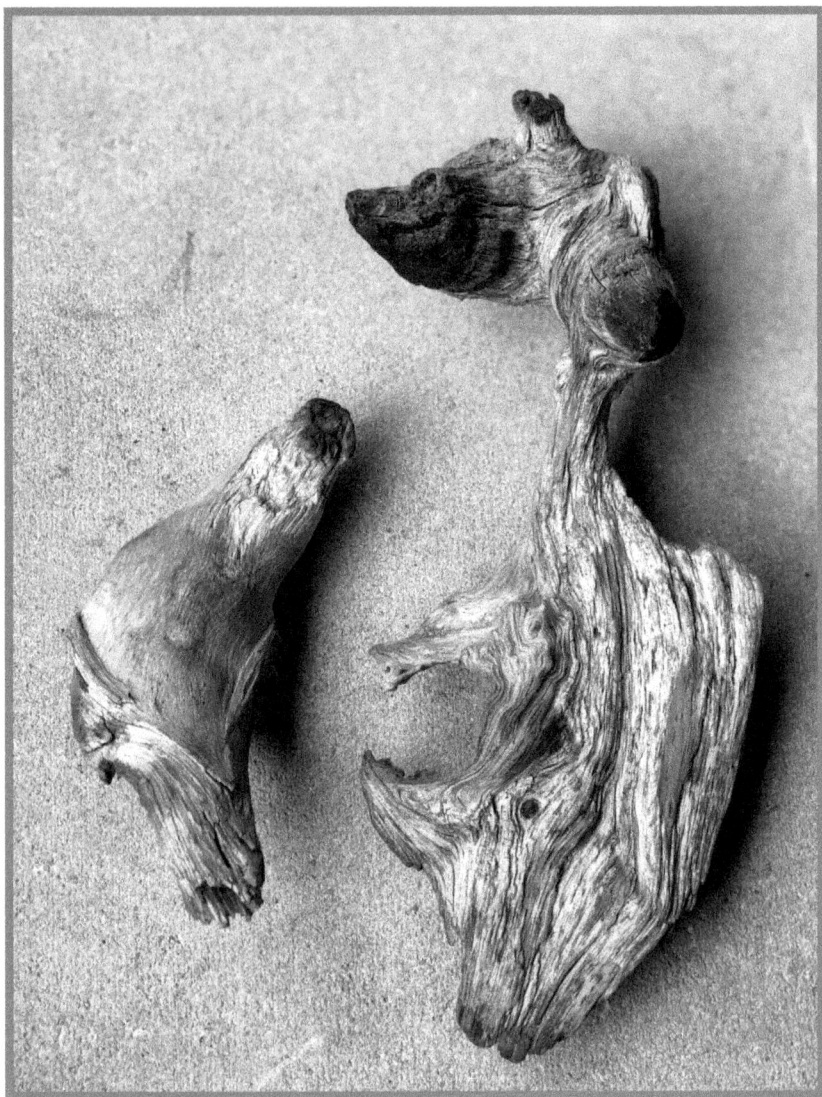

He and She - Found objets d' art
Inspiration for *She Speaks and Body Matters*
♂ 4" ♀ 7"
Driftwood

238

She Speaks
Mono-print, ink and acrylic on paper
32"x20"

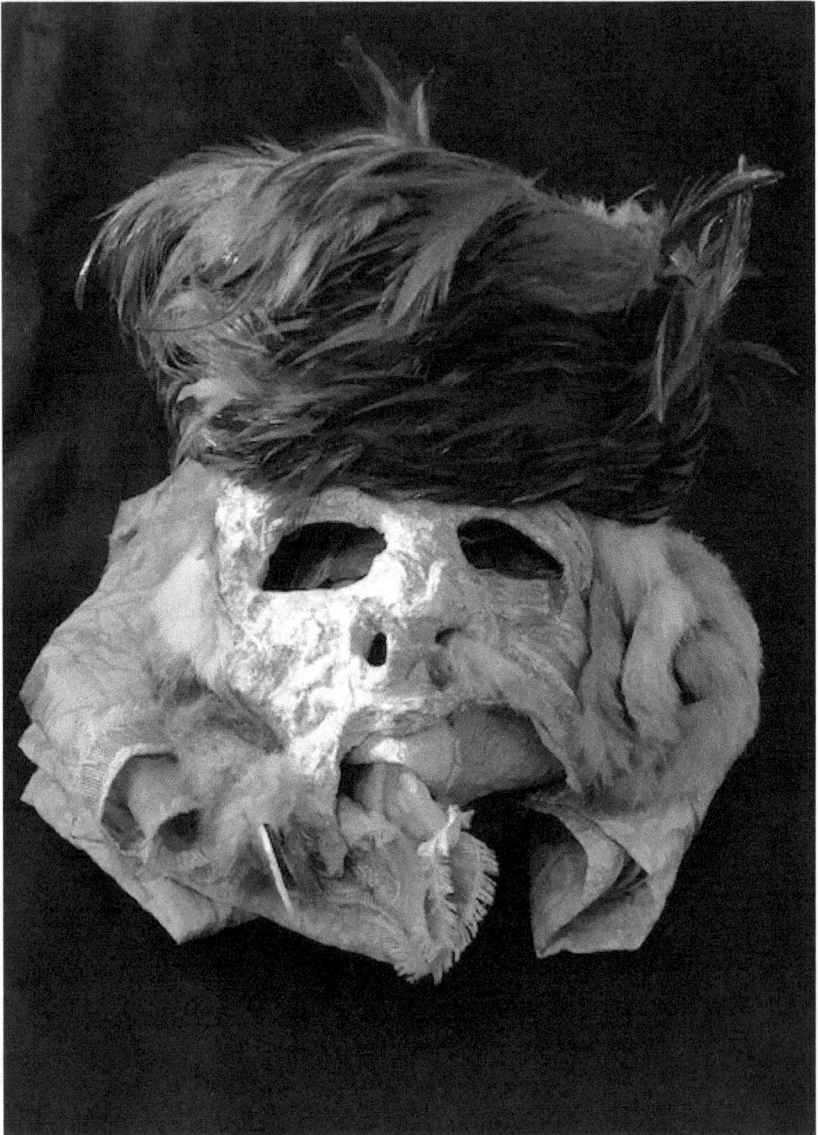

Animal Urges
Papier-mâché mask
Fur and fabric

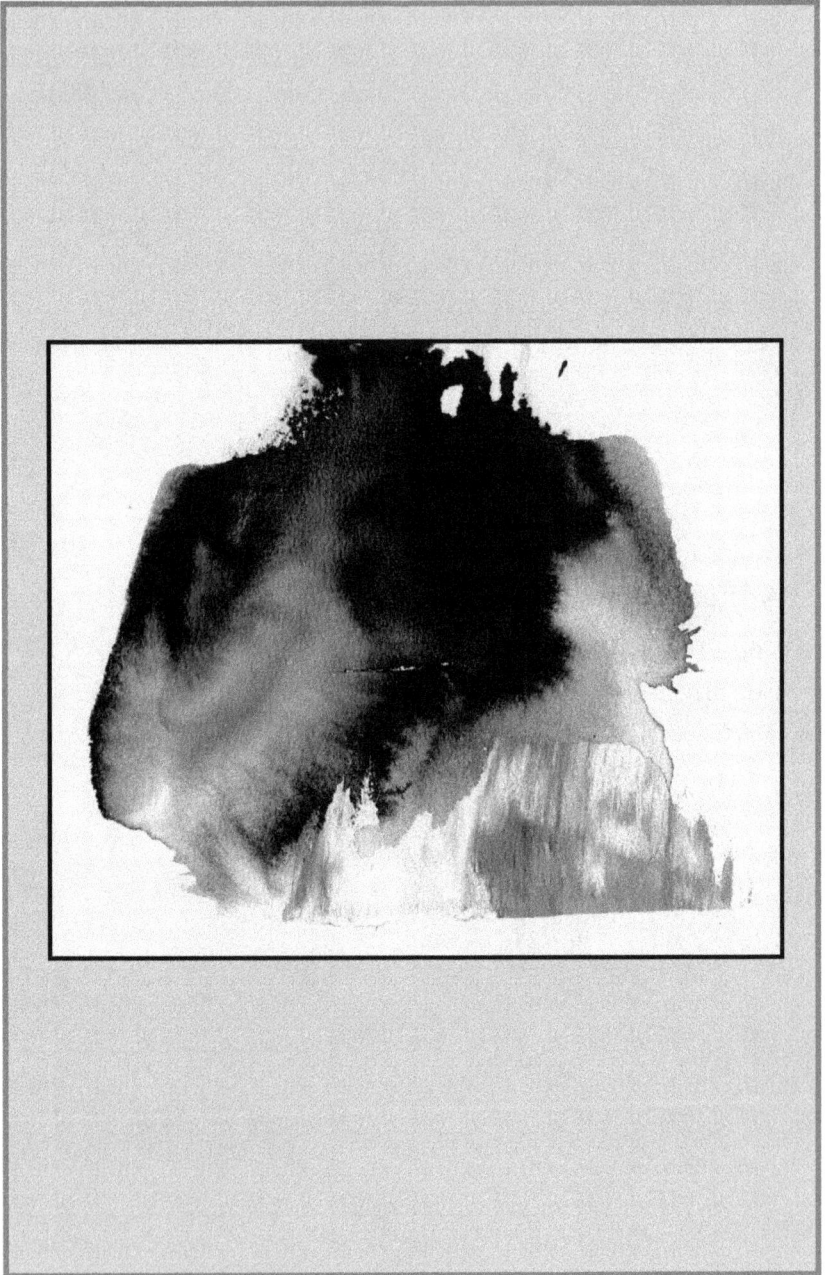

Burning Torso
8"x10"
Ink and acrylic on paper

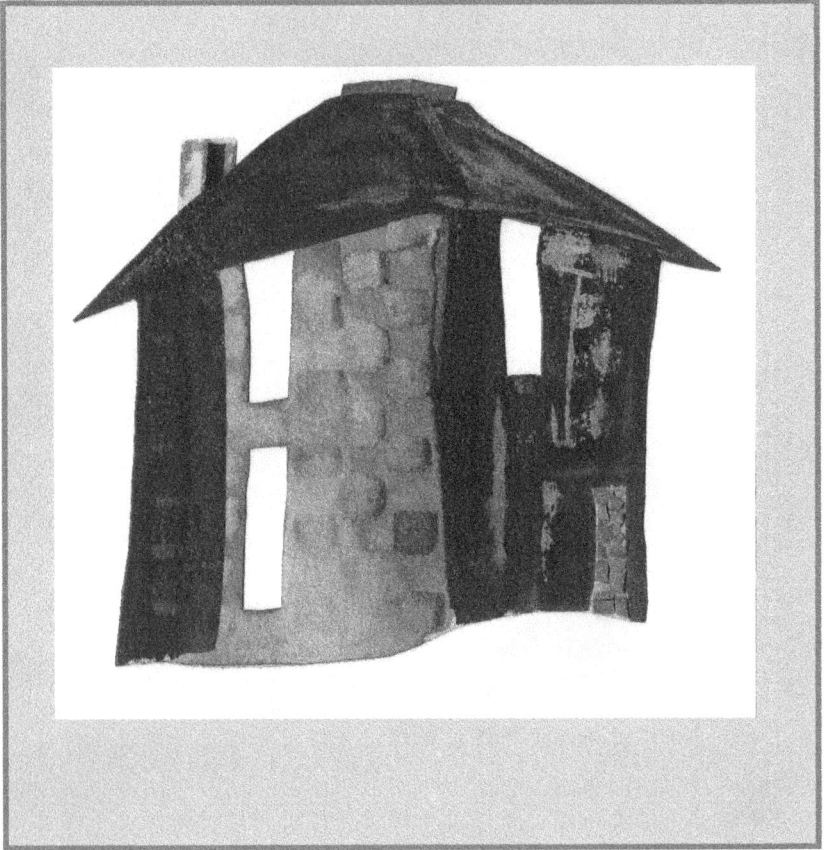

Abandoned, But Not Empty
8"x10"
Mixed media on paper

Fledgling
8"x10"
Ink and acrylic on paper

Body Matters
32"x20"
Mono-print, ink and acrylic on paper

Milkweed
5'x3'
Acrylic on canvas

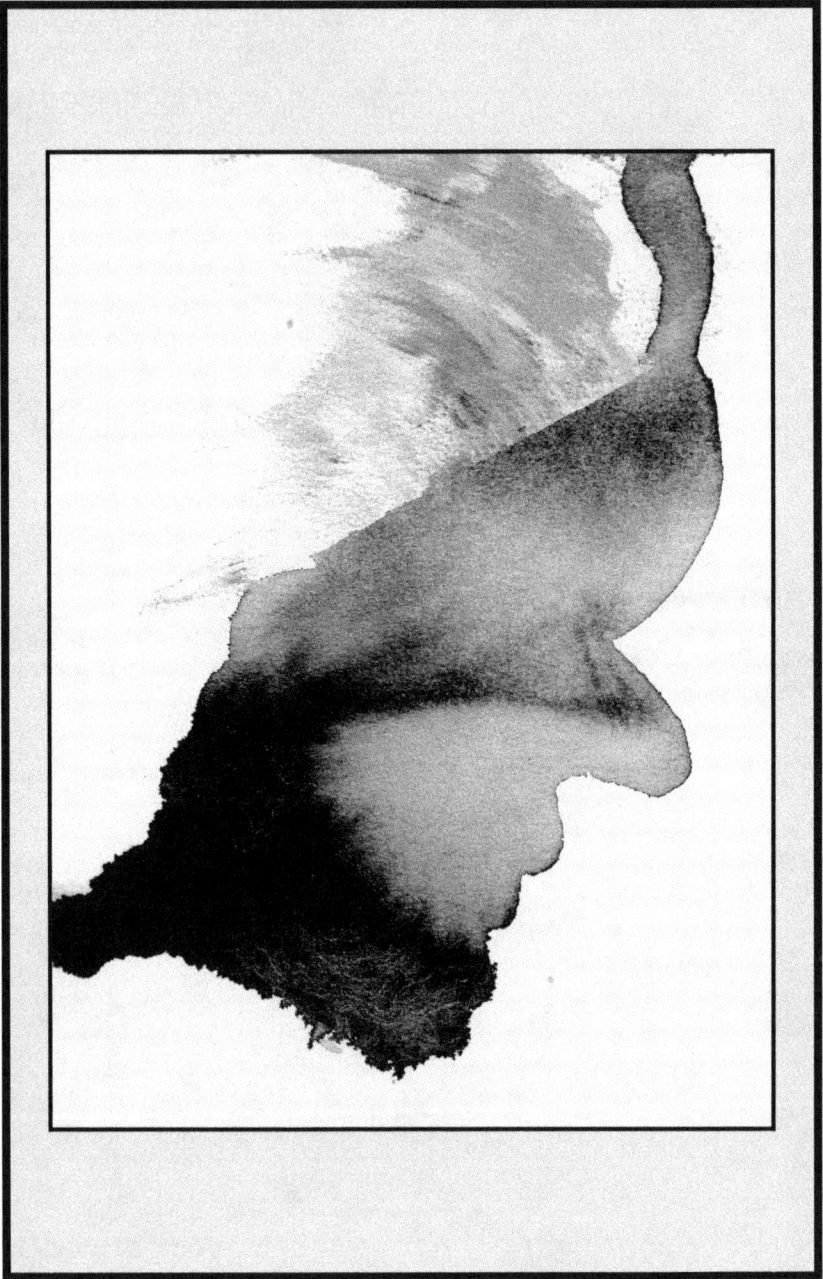

Infinite Mind
8"x10"
Ink and acrylic on paper

Index

Alfred Wolfsohn 204, 205

Brené Brown 47

Carl Jung 206

Cy Twombly 46, 211

Danny Grossman 147

Denial 7

Diamond Heart 137

Dr. Pat Ogden 92

Dr. Richard Schwartz 91

Jerome Frank 202

Joseph Campbell 202

Karen Kain 147

Nick Ortner 224

Psychodramatic Bodywork 92

Richard Schwartz 59

Roy Hart 206

Rudolf Laban 115

Susan Aaron 92

Big Mind 71

Byron Katie 126, 224

Continuum 19

Dean Gilmour 23

Donna Eden 129, 135, 224

Eckhart Tolle 194

Emily Conrad 19, 133

Genpo Roshi 72

Impulse, definition 18
Internal Family Systems Therapy (IFS) 166, 184
Jim Warren 23
Linda Putnam 102, 116
Maxim Mazumdar 165
Noh Theatre 23
Reptilian Brain 122
Richard Pochinko 23
Richard Schwartz, Dr. 56, 189
Rickie Wold 23
Rorschach Test 131
Shock 7
Sorrow, defined 161
Trauma 7, 17, 59
Ushio Shinohara 65
Wildebeest 7
York University 8, 15